Leah

LENS of FAITH

Everything changed the day I got on my knees and surrendered all

LENS OF FAITH

LENS OF FAITH PUBLISHING COMPANY

Lens of Faith book

Lens of Faith® Ministries registered in the United States Patent and Trademark Office 2020

Includes bibliographical references.

ISBN 979-8-9916556-0-6 (softcover)

All Scripture quotations, unless otherwise indicated, are taken from The Holy Bible, New International Version®, NIV®. Copyright © 1973, 1978, 1984, 2011 Bible Gateway, Inc. ® All rights reserved worldwide. The "NIV" and "New International Version" are trademarks registered in the United States Patent and Trademark Office by Bible Gateway® a division of The Zondervan Corporation, 501 Nelson Pl, Nashville, TN 37214 USA

Cover design: Leah Carson
Author photo: myconfidentstyle.com

LEAHMARIECARSON.COM

Copyright © 2022 Leah Carson

All rights reserved.

DEDICATION

This book is an act of pure devotion and obedience to my everything, Jesus Christ. Without him I would not have this story to share with you. May my life continue to display his wonders and bring him great glory here on earth.

Thank you to those that continue to believe, encourage and pray for me on this journey. You know who you are. I'm forever grateful for your unwavering support.

CONTENTS

1 THE GOOD, THE BAD AND THE UGLY   pg 1

2 WHAT'S NEXT?   pg 27

3 UNHEALTHY ATTRACTS UNHEALTHY   pg 39

4 BEAUTIFUL SURRENDER   pg 47

5 CRAZY FAITH   pg 65

6 GOD'S PERSPECTIVE   pg 89

7 RADICAL OBEDIENCE   pg 105

8 FRUIT OF THE WILDERNESS   pg 135

9 DON'T GIVE UP   pg 181

10 LIVE YOUR BEST LIFE   pg 187

BONUS:
SPIRITUAL WARFARE PRAYER   pg 191

INTRODUCTION

For those of you who are trusting and waiting for specific promises from God to be fulfilled in your life, I wrote this book for you.

For those who need hope and God's perspective in a time of increasing pain and loss, this is for you.

For those of you who need greater faith to believe that all things are possible with God, this is for you.

I hope to encourage you in whatever circumstance you are facing. We serve a mighty God who hasn't lost his power. If he can use me to display his wonders, then he can do the same for you. He is just waiting for your yes.

Do you know that it is impossible to please God without faith?

> "Now faith is being sure of what we hope for and certain of what we do not see. This is what the ancients were honored for. Without faith it is impossible to please God." -Hebrews 11

Faith is mentioned 270 times in the Word of God. This is because every epic Bible story required a man or a woman to trust God, to walk in faith and costly obedience.

"Walk by Faith, not by sight." -2 Corinthians 5:7

You need great faith to keep your joy in opposition, endure adversity, and to believe God even when the evidence is stacked against you.

I have always been a faithful person, but never have I been tested in my faith like in these past eleven years.

LOOKING BACK

Like many, I thought that I was a "good enough" Christian. I served in my local church, gave my 10% and surrounded myself with a supportive community. But I lived in full independence mode as if I was saying, "I love you Jesus, but I got this."

And while it is true that so many others looked up to me and my walk, God still did not have the one thing that he values most: my whole heart.

Little did I know, God was about to flip my comfortable world upside down. Everything was about to drastically change and I would never be the same.

Buckle up friends, this is a wild ride.

CHAPTER 1

THE GOOD, THE BAD AND THE UGLY

Growing up, I would half-jokingly say, "I'm never getting married" and "I'm never having kids." My family and friends still remember this well. I know most girls look forward to the opposite, getting married and having children but I had a distorted view of both.

The reason that I made such reckless and immature statements was because for so long, I did not know of many "happy" marriages or parents. When I was around married couples, there was often a lack of friendship, romance and/or respect. Then I would spend time with a variety of different parents who always seemed stressed and looking for a way of escape.

Later my mom tells me,

"God doesn't put two people together to make them happy, he does it to make them holy."

I instantly rejected that idea, of course. What young girl wants to hear that God isn't here to make her happy?

Then one day during a church service, someone prayed that, "God's will would be done in my life." I didn't want that. I thought if God had his way, I would be miserable. It was during that church service that he pointed me to the scripture verse, Jeremiah 29:11.

> "For I know the plans I have for you," declares the Lord, "plans to prosper you and not to harm you, plans to give you hope and a future."

It was in that moment, that God started to soften my heart regarding his will and marriage. He started to reveal himself to me as a perfect Father.

God is not out to get you. His goal isn't to make you miserable - in fact just the opposite is true. Then God began to deal with me on speaking against having children. Let me just say, I was not the girl that dreamt of being a mom.

Blame it on the challenges of having a large family and the responsibilities that come with being the oldest of eight siblings. Let's not forget all of the babysitting jobs from other families, starting when I was thirteen years old. I'm laughing right now because I remember needing a long break from children.

Don't get me wrong, I love kids. And I'm definitely a loving, protective and fun aunt to all ten of my nieces and nephews now. But at that time, I wanted what I never had, which was my own quiet space.

In fact, when I was twenty-one years old, I got my own apartment and was set on not getting a roommate. I would say, "I don't want to share my stuff. I want my own bathroom and I don't want anybody to steal my clothes." That was a half joke. If you have sisters, you get it. Well, let's just say you have five sisters and two brothers like I do, now you really get it.

But then in my mid-twenties, I had a divine encounter at a church event where God sternly corrected me,

"Stop speaking against what I have for you. My plans for you are good."

One of the great things that my parents instilled in all of us, is the fear of the Lord. When he corrects me, it's like, yes sir.

So in that moment when he got my attention, I repented and renounced any word curses that I have ever spoken over myself and my future that were in opposition to God's will for my life. After he dealt with me, I began to desire marriage. Although, I have been in a total of three serious relationships, they all led to heartbreak instead of going down the aisle.

PRINCE CHARMING

After my last dating relationship, I remained single, pure and waited for "the one" for several years. It was a sweet season in my life as I grew in my faith and was part of an awesome young adult church community. It was there that I met some of my closest friends, still to this day.

I hoped to meet my love match, but there was absolutely no one on my radar in whom I had any interest.

But that all changed when I was thirty-four years old and I met a charming Southern boy named Robert. A friend convinced me to try online dating, even though I was very hesitant, I signed up and shortly after I met Robert. He was driving across the country to work a summer job at his uncle's company in my home state. It felt like I was also on the adventure as he'd share his many discoveries with me along the way. He'd eagerly call me like, "They have the best steak here in Texas!"

He quickly swept me off my feet with his boyish charm and sense of adventure. Robert was different than any guy I had ever met, and we instantly hit it off. He checked off many of my boxes on paper. Christian. Respectful. Kind. Spontaneous.

But while we were on one of our first dates, I saw red flag number one. It was the fourth of July and we were excited to celebrate by going to watch a fireworks show; I even invited two of my sisters to join us. As we were parking at a public viewing spot, a man got furious and went off on Robert for parking too close to him.

They both ended up in an uncontrollable shouting match. I was humiliated, especially with my sisters being there to witness the way my date reacted.

This chaotic scene was telling. On our drive back to my home after the fireworks, I told him, "I don't want to date a man with an anger problem." My last boyfriend had an anger problem and I didn't want to repeat that mistake. Robert was quiet and you could tell that he felt bad. The next day, he showed up on my doorstep with a three-page apology letter that he had written. "I was walking the park and asking God for forgiveness. I'm sorry. I'll never get angry like that again." he says.

He was so sweet and apologetic that I gave him another chance. I really liked so many other traits about him.

When he said he "would never get angry like that again", I wanted to believe him and so I did.

We moved past the insult and spent every day of that summer together. Our same love for spontaneous adventures, good food, light-hearted fun and community made many picture-perfect memories.

We even drove back to his home state, across the country together for one of his work trips. It was good times.

My entire family and all of my friends approved of my boyfriend. "You met your match! You and Robert are so good together. He's great." they said. Not one of them had anything negative to say.

Even though Robert acted out in bad behavior at times while we were dating, I reasoned it with the fact that nobody is perfect. And my mental list told me that his good outweighed the bad. I still believed that this man was the answer to my prayers.

The overwhelming amount of adoration for him and for us as a couple was confirmation, that we were meant to be.

Everybody loved us together, except his mother who has a history of being possessive of her only son and jealous of any woman that he's ever dated.

She also struggles with bitterness stemming from her past and now being married to her third husband, who is an alcoholic. This gave me a better understanding on why Robert acted the way he did at times.

Robert later tells me that he called his mom after our second date full of excitement, "I found the girl I'm going to marry!"

He dated a variety of women but never wanted to get married until he met me. His mother in shock, jumped on the first flight to come meet me. It wasn't a warm welcome. I soon discovered that Robert would get easily triggered by his mother, which made me feel sorry for him.

It is very important to consider the relatives of the person you intend to marry. Who they are can impact your marriage, more than you may realize. Someone else's family can be a wonderful addition to your life or a destructive one.

I had hoped that his mother and I would build a great relationship, but that was not the case. Still Robert and I continued to date and fall in love. We talked about marriage and what a possible future together would look like.

After courting for just five months, Robert asked me to marry him and he was quite persistent. One night he tells me, "When you find the one you want to spend the rest of your life with, you want the rest of your life to start right away." What a line.

This was all happening a bit too soon for me, but it's also what I wanted. My main concern was me being the spiritual leader. There was also the concern I had when we would go out to eat and he would order three beers for himself. The only reason somebody would consume three drinks, is to get drunk.

But again, I would reason that he had so many Christ-like attributes and that he would grow spiritually over time.

There's a saying that goes:

"A woman marries a man expecting him to change and a man marries a woman expecting her to never change."

Which means, women often choose a mate who needs help but has good potential, because they tend to have a fix-it attitude. Like, I'll fix it later or after we get married, he'll change. The opposite is true for men.

A man will meet a woman when she's at her best. Then they expect her to stay that way throughout marriage. Stay the same weight, look the same, act the same and such. Both of these ideas give you unrealistic expectations in relationships.

Don't make a decision based on someone's potential, instead look at their *patterns*.

There are many things to love about Robert, such as his tender and generous heart. There were times that he would empty his wallet for the homeless or for a charity without anyone knowing about it. He would go out of his way to serve a person in need. He's even risked his life for others that were in harm's way. Like the time he ran out in the middle of a hurricane to help firefighters move fallen trees away from the road. Or the time, he ran into a burning building to rescue a family.

That happened one day when we were helping friends move. Suddenly, we saw an apartment in the complex engulfed in flames. Robert bravely ran into the burning building, without hesitation, and rescued the family that was trapped in the apartment. The firefighters showed up on the scene and were amazed. They were so impressed, that they offered him a job.

Who wouldn't want to marry a brave man that impresses fire fighters, right ladies!

When Robert asked me to marry him, I didn't take long to answer Yes. He convinced me that he was the perfect man for me and that our lives would be wonderful together. He even swore so on his most treasured possession, which is his grandfather's Bible.

I thought we were starting off right. Robert not only properly asked my dad for my hand in marriage but my entire family and all my friends approved. Unlike my past boyfriends, with Robert, everyone was thrilled and gave us their blessing.

We honored each other and God by staying completely pure before marriage. We took a different route then going through traditional pre-marital counseling. Instead, we both individually took our time and finished the pre-marital study guide, "101 Questions to Ask Before You Get Engaged". This book covers every topic and question to prepare you for a healthy marriage. As we sat down to discuss the questions and answers together, we were in agreement. This seemed like another sign that we were meant for each other.

After a short courtship, we planned our wedding. Our October wedding celebration was dreamy, complete with a horse and carriage at a historic farm in my hometown. Seventy of our closest loved ones, beaming with joy, cheered us on as we became husband and wife. It really was a fairytale come true.

We had a romantic first night together, where my husband filled our hotel room with rose petals and my favorite candles. The very next morning he whisked me away to a vacation home in the mountains to enjoy our honeymoon.

I was excited for this new chapter in our life and ready to devote myself to Robert as his wife.

Going back to when we were dating, we discussed what our marriage would look like. We both agreed to move across the country to his home state right after our honeymoon, so that he could finish earning his business degree.

Then after one year, our plan was to move back to my home state indefinitely. That is where I already had an established home, family and a community eager for our return. At the time he acted as if it was a great plan. He also assured me that he would have no problem relocating from his beloved home state and far from his parents, despite being their only child.

REALITY CHECK

The very next day after our honeymoon, we moved across the country and into our first home together. It was then that I got a reality check.

On one hand, Robert showed his tenderness like writing me cute love notes every morning before he went to work and surprising me with fun date nights.

On the other hand, he would act out of irrational jealousy, anger and showed controlling behavior. His mother was also eager to cause conflict and division when she had the chance. It is true that hurt people; hurt people. His childhood friends even corrected him for the way he treated me at times. This all left me disappointed and with unmet expectations early on in our marriage. In turn, I lacked the empathy, quick forgiveness and the grace that my husband desired.

EMOTIONAL SOUL WOUNDS

I now know firsthand that unhealed emotional soul wounds will lead to a variety of issues, such as depression and addiction. Even though Robert and I have similar interests and values, we both have very different backgrounds and family dynamics.

Growing up in my family, there was no tolerating or enabling certain behavior and my father was quick to discipline. My parents both had godless alcoholic fathers but they both got radically saved by Jesus Christ at nineteen years old. This is why they don't touch alcohol or even coffee to this day. My dad would say, "I don't want any addictions in our home." It's funny but even now he doesn't like that I love a good cup of coffee each morning.

All of the rules growing up seemed a bit extreme, especially as a teenager. Being raised in such an environment taught me intolerance of certain issues.

My upbringing came with its own challenges but addiction wasn't one of them. Robert however, was raised in a home with an alcoholic parent and was enabled. An alcoholic household often creates an environment where emotional expression is unacceptable or ignored, so children adopt the habit of hiding emotions. As adults they may be at higher risk for depression, neglecting health-care routines, and feelings of loneliness. Fear other people, authority figures, and anger.

On a positive note, his parents have always been very financially generous towards him, and he was in turn generous to others.

It's important when you are dating or getting to know someone, that you also get to know their background. Quite often, that will tell you what to expect in the future.

Despite the disappointments in our marriage, we both loved each other and had good times as a couple. Others would call us, "The life of the party."

We enjoyed spontaneous trips to the beach, the mountains and everywhere in between. We were also committed to a good church and part of a godly community, where we built solid relationships.

I was however concerned that Robert's core closest friends from childhood, were not Christians. They disrespected women, had foul mouths and were drinkers. I didn't understand then why he spent so much time with these men. But as the saying goes, birds of a feather flock together. Show me your friends, I'll show you your future.

> "Walk with the wise and become wise for a companion of fools suffers harm." -Proverbs 13:20

Whether for ill or good, the companions we choose will have a strong influence on us. Choose wise friends and in doing so you will set the trajectory for your own decisions and character.

Robert and I moved directly after our honeymoon to his hometown so that he could finish his degree but once we were settled, he decided not to complete his studies. He reasoned that because he had a good job, he didn't need to graduate. This revealed a much deeper issue. Since adulthood, he has had a pattern of giving up when faced with adversity and often takes the easy way out when he feels overwhelmed. People will show what they are made of in times of adversity.

After one year we followed through with our plan to move back to my home state. Robert was given a work position and everything was set in place. So, we packed up the truck and then stopped by his parents to say goodbye. As we drove off, he suddenly pulls over to the side of the road where he has a complete emotional breakdown.

I was stunned and not sure what to do. But as my husband was weeping, I realized **he is not ready for this.**

But here we are packed and ready to go. So we continued on our journey and made the most of our trip filled with fun spontaneous stops. Robert came up with such a good idea. "You're a great Photographer. We should stop along the way so you can take photos of barns and make a coffee table book." So I did. That is a great memory and I still have the book I designed.

After our long drive across the map, we arrived and settled into what was once my home but now our home. Everything started off on the right foot but those unresolved issues began to surface and his depression and drinking escalated. To make it worse, Robert was not honest enough with himself to even admit he had a problem.

My husband would take off to bars to watch sports, get drunk and then crash on our couch, whenever he wanted. I was determined to not repeat his parents' marriage of an alcoholic husband and a bitter wife, so I put my foot down.

One night when he came home drunk, I told him he could not take off to bars, come home drunk at all hours of the night, crash on the couch and also stay in our home. He then chose to leave and move in with his co-worker. What I really wanted was for Robert to get help. To get right with God and to make our marriage his priority, but he was unable. My husband was emotionally immature and not ready for the commitment that is needed in marriage.

These are signs that someone is emotionally immature:

- Avoid hard conversations
- Be very self-centered
- Be overly reactive and throw adult tantrums
- Be stuck in an unresolved trauma cycle at the age when the trauma happened
- Blame you and others for their problems
- Name call and not fight fair in arguments
- Refuse to do their own internal work
- Not self-reflect
- Keep conversations on a surface level only
- Drain your energy because of their neediness and childlike behavior

I have learned that no matter how much you want, pray and pressure someone to change, ultimately, they must want it for themselves. The enemy, who is the devil, keeps emotionally and spiritually weak people deceived, bound and broken. They remain this way until they allow Jesus Christ to bring them the healing and deliverance they need. Only God's spirit and power can truly change a person.

> "People will show you what they are made of in times of *adversity.*"

ON THE ROCKS

My husband had spiraled into a depression that caused him to drink more heavily and have angry outbursts. Instead of fighting for our marriage, he was fighting demons that were warring for his soul.

Robert began living as if he was single shortly after we separated. As he was staying with his co-worker; he fell apart and told me that he believed our marriage was over. Instead of taking responsibility for his drinking, he played the victim and his mother shamed me for "kicking him out." She told me once, "You join a support group for yourself, and deal with it."

We were intentionally created with a God-shaped hole, that only he can fill. Nothing else can truly satisfy that void. My husband repeated a lifelong pattern: any time life got too hard he would quit. He would dismiss whatever was challenging him and then go and chase after the next new thing. It's an endless pursuit of happiness that can never be met until you are truly surrendered to Christ.

We still would spend time together, but our marriage was hanging on by a thread. Then after a couple months of separation, we suddenly got news that Robert's job was relocating him to another state. We just moved to our home a year earlier and now we had to move again, but this time our marriage was on the rocks. I found out later that it was actually his mother who put in the call to his employer to have him transferred, hoping I would stay behind. But we stayed together.

We felt forced to move to this small town, in the middle of nowhere surrounded by corn fields with no family, friends and a failing marriage.

We tried to start fresh but Robert was not content in any area of his life and he still held onto resentment from our past. In addition, his mental health and drinking were out of control.

I was hurting and feeling helpless.

Just as before, Robert was taking off to local bars at night, to watch sports and get drunk. I never knew at what time he would stumble in the front door. I told him that I didn't want this for us and that he needed help. I even found a local faith-based addiction recovery program for my husband. He went one time but then came home saying, "Those people are worse off than me. I don't need to go back."

Denial is when someone ignores, downplays, or distorts reality. When a person continues to lie to themselves then they cannot take the next step needed to change: admitting is the first step to recovery. Denial will keep you stuck.

It was difficult for me to have the empathy that he said he needed and to keep my cool in that toxic environment. Feeling helpless, I would get angry and say unkind things. Sadly, I was losing respect for the man that I loved. I kept hoping and praying for him and for us but instead of a turnaround, things got worse.

THE BREAKING POINT

One late night, while Robert was out drinking, I sat on the couch in the dark, feeling alone and hopeless. Suddenly, I saw flashing red lights outside our living room window. I looked out to see my husband being pulled over for drunk driving as he was on his way home. He was being belligerent with the police officer and then got arrested, but was released that evening. He later stumbled in apologizing to me and then crashed on the bed.

My husband got arrested, got a DUI, lost his license and his job all in one swoop. I was hoping that this would be the wake up call he desperately needed. That he would recognize his drinking was jeopardizing our marriage and causing him harm. Instead, just a couple days later, he tail spun into manic mode and went right back into drinking uncontrollably.

That was the last straw for me. Robert told me that we would have to move in with his parents and I said, no. He replied with, "I understand but I have to." As he continued to spiral, I told him I can't do this anymore.

That was just what his mother was hoping to hear. She then drove eight hours to pick up Robert and pack up her car with his belongings. She did all this without even acknowledging me. Before she left, she ripped a scripture on forgiveness off of our wall.

Robert felt defeated as he kissed me one last time on my forehead and said, "I have no dignity. You deserve better. You should be married to a pastor." Then just like that, he walked out of my life.

I just stood there stunned and in disbelief as he left out the door. It has been over ten years since that day and that was the last time that I saw my husband.

RELEASE THEM

Even though my husband and mother-in-law have caused me pain, I choose to forgive and bless them. The word of God says, "bless those that curse you." I know! Easier said than done. But this powerful habit will keep your heart soft. Forgiveness prevents the devil from gaining ground in your life. Don't give him access. It doesn't matter who is wrong or who is right. It is not worth holding onto.

Forgiveness is a choice. Everything in our nature tells us to blame others and deny forgiveness. But God tells us to forgive even when we don't want to.

Keep forgiving over and over. Never stop releasing offense. From the beginning and to this day, I choose to forgive and pray for what matters most: their surrender to Jesus Christ. I pray that they will have an undeniable encounter with the true living God. Jesus loves them more than I ever could and he wants the prodigals to come home.

People will always disappoint you because we live in a broken world and nobody is perfect. It's important to watch what comes out of your mouth when you are faced with an offense. Speak words of life not death, even when it doesn't feel good or seem true. Ask God to help you to see your offender the way he sees them. Call that forth. I know this is a challenge but it can be done. The more that you understand that word curses have powerful consequences and give permission to the enemy, the more you will think before you speak.

Unforgiveness and speaking word curses are two of the main things that will give the enemy legal rights to bring an accusation against you. It is important to be careful of these traps. It's not worth it. Let it go. Holding onto offense poisons your soul. Don't partner with the devil, he is the one that wants to defeat you. Silence the accuser. Partner with the Prince of Peace, he is the one that wants to set you free to live victoriously. Declare God's truth and speak life in every situation.

"The one who guards his mouth preserves his life; the one who opens wide his lips comes to ruin."

-Proverbs 13:3

"The words of the reckless pierce like swords, but the tongue of the wise brings healing." -Proverbs 12:18

"For if you forgive others their trespasses, your heavenly Father will also forgive you, but if you do not forgive others their trespasses, neither will your Father forgive your trespasses." -Matthew 6:14-15

> "We were intentionally created with a *God-shaped* hole, that only he can fill."

CHAPTER 2

WHAT'S NEXT?

I truly loved my husband and I strongly believe that marriage is a covenant that is established and honored by God. I do not take this covenant lightly. I have watched my parents navigate through the darkest storms in their marriage together and they are still married, going on forty-nine years.

Of course, no one wants a failed marriage. I wanted him get the help he needed, but that's not what happened.

After my husband said goodbye, I was in a state of shock. I had no family or friends in the state to turn to and I was left to pack up our huge Victorian home and move out quickly. I sold almost everything. A flight attendant friend took a week off work to help me load up a Uhaul truck with the remaining belongings.

That day, my childhood friend looks over at me and says, "I have never seen you like this." I was reeling from the breakup and was in survival mode.

Lord, what now?

I knew that I was at a very critical life-altering crossroad. Do I go back home where my family, friends and familiarity are or do I head in the opposite direction of my husband? My path was made clear. Even though Robert told me not to contact him, I felt led to relocate to the same city.

At this point, I was also believing God for great things to take place in our marriage. I will go more into detail in the chapter, Crazy Faith. So with the moving truck packed up, I got behind the wheel and by God's grace made it to my destination. What was God up to?

GOD'S WAYS ARE HIGHER

I wanted God to make sense of this. Why was I here, alone and separated from all that mattered to me? I always said that, "I would never leave my family and never leave my home state." Well never tell God never.

His plan included me doing everything that I said, "I would never do."

When my life fell apart, God led me across the country far from my loved ones and far from everything familiar to me. I was homesick, broken hearted and feeling alone at rock bottom. I cried out to God asking him,

"Why did you move me here, across the country, in a different culture, alone and far from my family and friends?"

His answer was, "You would never be who I've called you to be, living fifteen minutes from your family, distracted and in your comfort zone. I brought you here to do a new thing in you. Not a revised version but a NEW THING. You will never be the same."

Sheesh.

At the time, everyone thought I moved to the same city as Robert to be near him but it was never about him. God led me here for an entirely different purpose. A greater purpose.

YOUR STORY FOR MY GLORY

When my husband walked out, I was devastated and didn't talk about my situation. But one night as I attended a Bible study God says, "I cannot get the glory from your story, if you won't share." It was then that I began sharing with everyone that I spent time with, starting that very night at the home group. Knowing that words are powerful, I've always been careful to not bash Robert or his mother. Instead, I take the opportunity to point to God's goodness and to share his future promises.

I know countless others can relate to a broken marriage, addiction, abandonment and rejection. Since I have experienced it myself, I can now minister to others with a level of compassion and understanding like never before. There is power in your testimony, it can literally change lives.

God wants to use your pain for his purposes. Nothing is wasted when placed in God's hands.

"What the enemy meant to destroy me, God has used for my good and for his purposes." -Genesis 50:20

ARE YOU KIDDING ME?

A year later, after no contact with my husband, God gave me an assignment. He told me to drive to his parents' home, where he was living, and confidently tell him, "You're my husband. It's time to come home."

Are you kidding me? I have not spoken to him in a year and he has a girlfriend. Just the idea of doing this brought me so much anxiety. My initial response was, "No way", but God would not let it go. I even got two prophetic confirmations that I needed to do this. And of course, I had no peace until I yielded to the assignment.

So out of obedience and with my heart pounding, I drove to Robert's parents' home. There were no cars in the driveway, so I started leaving his neighborhood. Then suddenly, I looked in my rear-view mirror to see my husband following me.

I knew that was an act of God, it was like he came out of nowhere. Robert then immediately called me on the phone to ask me what I wanted. After some small talk, with confidence I said exactly how and what the Lord directed me to say, "You're my husband. It's time to come home."

He mockingly laughed at me and said no. But as I drove out of his neighborhood, I had such a feeling of peace as I sensed God's good pleasure rush over me. I was hoping that by this outrageous act of obedience, God would have done an instant miracle to soften Robert's heart and he would return to me then. But that didn't happen.

God requires us to obey him no matter what the outcome. No matter how we may feel and even when we don't fully understand.

Sometimes after an act of obedience, we will see God perform a sudden and powerful turn around in our situation. But there are other times when we won't get any instant gratification except for the peace that always comes with obedience. In fact, sometimes our situation may even seem to get worse. This is why we really need to trust the Lord completely. Proverbs 3:5-6 tells us,

"Trust in the Lord with all your heart and lean not on your own understanding; in all your ways submit to him and he will make your paths straight."

I did not understand why God had me go to my husband and boldly declare that he return. In fact, instead of my situation turning around, it seemed to get worse. After a year being separated, Robert located my address and sent me bad news. When the police officer

knocked on my door that day, he had a sad look on his face as he handed me divorce papers and said, "I'm sorry." Somehow, I knew immediately what he was sorry about and what the papers were. As soon as I opened the legal documents, I heard God clearly tell me,
"Don't sign anything. You will not partner with him in his rebellion."

So, I never signed anything and never needed a lawyer or a court date. Being completely detached in that way has also helped prevent the additional pain that often comes with that entire legal process.

God constantly reminds me that what may feel like rejection, is actually his protection.
"It's not rejection, it's my protection." says the Lord.

Obedience requires commitment! God requires us to partner with him and obey- the results are up to him. We have to stay committed to trusting our trustworthy and faithful heavenly Father, with any and all outcomes.

God is **Sovereign**.

The Bible tells us over and over that God's ways are not our ways and that his ways are much higher. So, if that's true than why do we continue to put the creator of

the universe in our logical human box? Why do we expect him to perform according to our very limited understanding?
Almighty God doesn't think like us and he doesn't move like us.

We tend to only see the chapter we are in but God sees the bigger picture. He knows the beginning, the middle and the end of our time on this earth and he is all in the details.

Your chapter may look painful or disappointing now but there is hope for the future and your story has purpose. Your life is not over.

God doesn't create mistakes. Your gender, your ethnicity and your age are all planned on purpose for a purpose.

> "For we are God's handiwork, created in Christ Jesus to do good works, which God prepared in advance for us to do." -Ephesians 2:10

There is a living God that knows the exact number of hairs on your head. Every detail concerning you matters to him. He is all in your business in a good way.

> "It's not rejection, it's my *protection*."

"For you Lord created my inmost being; you knit me together in my mother's womb. I praise you because I am fearfully and wonderfully made; your works are wonderful, I know that full well. Your eyes saw my unformed body; all the days ordained for me were written in your book before one of them came to be. How precious to me are your thoughts, God. How vast is the sum of them! Were I to count them, they would outnumber the grains of sand - when I awake, I am still with you." -Psalm 139

Trust the Author of your life story. Trust his timing. Trust his ways. Trust his perfect character. Trust his love. God is trustworthy because he is true.

LENS OF FAITH

CHAPTER 3

UNHEALTHY ATTRACTS UNHEALTHY

When Robert walked out of our marriage, I was devastated. I rented out a small one-bedroom apartment, kept my boxes packed up and isolated myself for a couple of months. My husband never even checked on me. It was literally just me clinging onto Jesus as I hit rock bottom.

You don't know that Jesus is all you need, until he is all you got.

Jesus was my *rock* at rock bottom.

I eventually started going to a local church which is about an hour's drive out of town. On Sunday morning, I'd sit in the low-lit sanctuary on the back row with easy access to the exit doors so I could leave before anyone noticed. Those that know me, would be shocked to hear this since I am such a relational extrovert, but that's how devastated I was.

At this church, the pastor's wife started back up a healing and deliverance ministry for women called, Reality Revealed. She prayed about every one that showed interest in order to make sure it was who God wanted for that season. I felt that I should attend. In order to keep the class intimate, the group was made up of less than ten women. I did not know any of them at the time but by the end we knew each better than most.

This isn't your average women's ministry; in fact, it is the most intense healing ministry that I know of. Being a church girl my entire life, I have been through deep classes such as Cleansing Streams, Healing of the Heart and others, but this was different.

The popular saying, "Time heals all wounds" is just not true. Time doesn't heal wounds; it just hides them. I know good Christians who are in their seventies but they still react from and deal with trauma that happened in their childhood. Emotional healing is needed in order to be whole. When wounds are not fully healed, they always manifest some way and somehow. Instead of keeping ourselves distracted by life, we need to face all the yuck. The rejection. The abuse. The abandonment. The disappointments. All of it. You must allow God to reveal and heal childhood trauma and every fractured area in your soul.

Jesus wasn't rejected, betrayed, whipped, tortured and nailed to a tree, just so that you would believe and say a simple prayer. He died to set you free. We are meant to be free to run this race, not limp all the way to the finish line.

"Jesus himself bore our sins in his body on the cross, so that we might die to sins and live for righteousness; by his wounds you have been healed. I have come that you may have life, and have it to the full. I came to bind up the brokenhearted and set the prisoners free."
-John 10:10, Isaiah 61:1, 1 Peter 2:24

The enemy's strategy however is to keep us bound all the while convincing us that we are free. He is a liar and the father of lies (John 8:44). That's how Jesus describes our enemy. You may not see him with your physical eyes, but the devil uses different tactics to try and defeat us. As the liar, deceiver, and thief, our enemy is quite skilled at messing with our minds. And he wants us silenced and sidelined-speaking up turns the table and silences him instead.

Our leader made it clear up front that staying silent was not an option. And we were required to share the painful details of our individual traumas to a room of complete strangers. We had to answer the hard questions honestly in order to get to the root issues and receive true healing of our emotional soul wounds.

Along with sharing our trauma, we also had serious homework to complete every week. For example, one exercise was to go home and write letters to our offender until we had a positive feeling about that person. Then we had to burn the letters over the fire while saying out loud, "I forgive you _____."

I know it sounds over the top but this action actually brought great release.

I'm telling you, this ministry was no joke, it's a healing boot camp for the heart and soul. Our leader who experienced her own childhood trauma and healing had one goal for this class and that was to get to the root. We all knew that we needed to make our own healing a priority and take the necessary steps to freedom.

I'll never forget the moment that changed my life.

As you can imagine, it was not easy for me to share my fresh and overwhelming loss and pain but it was my turn. That Sunday, I was sitting at the table with all eyes on me as I was sharing with these women.

"It's his fault that our marriage fell apart. It was his drinking, his mother and his depression. He chose to walk out and abandon our marriage." I said.

I hoped for some sympathy but instead our leader unmoved, stops me in my tracks.

She looks me straight in my eyes and says, "Unhealthy attracts unhealthy."

I was quick to defend myself as I spouted out,

"He's the one with the issues. He walked out. I'm not perfect but this is his fault."

"No Leah! Unhealthy attracts unhealthy." She firmly says as she stares right into my soul.

I was taken back and speechless.

Isn't this how it usually goes when there is a breakup of any kind? We tend to blame the other person instead of looking inward.

After the class ended that day, I started on my hour drive back home. My natural response would have been to have a prideful attitude all while convincing myself that she doesn't know me, him or our marriage than dismiss what she said.

But the Holy Spirit would not let it go. Those words kept ringing in my spirit. He kept repeating what she said and would not stop the entire drive home.

"Unhealthy attracts *unhealthy.*"

CHAPTER 4

BEAUTIFUL SURRENDER

As soon as I got back to my apartment that Sunday afternoon, I sat on my couch to reason this all out with God.

"I think she's wrong, she doesn't know me or our marriage but if there's even 1% of truth to what she said, then show me" I said.

"Until you allow me to uproot the pride that runs deep in your family, you will never become the woman I have called you to be." He clearly responded.

I immediately dropped from my couch, hit my knees to the floor, stretched out my arms and said,

"Then Do it Lord. Do whatever you want to do in me. I'm yours."

Suddenly, I sensed a host of angels gathering over my left shoulder rejoicing and saying, "We have waited your entire life for this moment."

After I gave him my will and my heart, God began to perform the necessary heart surgery.

The truth is, many Christians live with Jesus as their Savior but not as their Lord.

JESUS TAKE THE WHEEL

I give this analogy, before I surrendered all to Christ, I was driving the car. He was my passenger, my buddy. I lived as if saying, "I love you Jesus but I got this." But when I truly surrendered all, I gave Jesus the wheel – now he is the driver. And I'm not even the passenger, instead, I sit in the back seat. I try to not be a back seat driver and ask God, "Where are we going?" or "Are we there yet?" Instead, I can look out the window and enjoy the journey because I trust the driver.

Friends, trust the driver. He will never get lost or arrive late. He will never crash. And he doesn't need a GPS!

"I have been crucified with Christ and I no longer live, but Christ lives in me. The life I now live in the body, I live by faith in the Son of God, who loved me and gave himself for me." -Galatians 2:20

There are many verses about surrendering all as a follower of Christ, such as this powerful commandment:

"Jesus tells his disciples, "If anyone would come after me, let him deny himself and take up his cross and follow me." -Matthew 16:24

This is obviously not a literal wooden cross like the one Jesus carried to calvary, to die for our sins. It's the cross of life. Your Comforts. Your Idols. Your Will. Your Plans. Your Sin. Anything that separates you and keeps you from completely following his perfect will for your life.

He died for it all and really, he deserves it all. No one deserves our devotion like King Jesus.

"Time doesn't heal wounds; it just *hides them.*"

UGLY PRIDE, BEAUTIFUL HUMILITY

We live in a culture that promotes and celebrates independence and pride, but God rejects every bit of it. He wants nothing to do with that independent, self-made, girl boss, selfish, all about me spirit which is driven by pride. He instead honors humility and dependence on him. The right view of yourself comes when you recognize that you are nothing apart from Jesus Christ. Every good attribute you have is because of who he is in you. It all points to him. He gets all the credit, and all the glory.

All throughout the Bible God warns us that, pride comes before a fall and that he hates it. God doesn't mention hating many things, but he literally hates pride because pride keeps his creation separated from him.

It was pride that got Lucifer kicked out of heaven. (Ezekiel 28)

"The arrogant cannot stand in your presence."
–Psalm 5:5

"I the Lord, hate pride and arrogance. I oppose a haughty attitude but I give grace to the humble."
-Proverbs 8:13

A religious spirit and a self-righteous attitude are rooted in pride. It is why the Pharisees were determined to have Jesus killed. We see the destruction that pride has caused throughout history.

I think that the most powerful example of pride and restoration in the Bible is the story of King Nebuchadnezzar.

He was a King who had it all. God favored him with fame, power, wealth and all his desires. Yet instead of praising God, he became arrogant and allowed his heart to harden.

God always warns us before we fall. In the King's case, he not only spoke to him through an upsetting dream but he also sent his Prophet. Daniel interpreted the dream which warned the King to repent before it was too late. God outlined exactly what would happen to him if he did not humble himself and renounce his sins.

Instead of humility, the King became more defiant. So it all came to pass. Everything God said would happen, in great detail, happened. He was driven away from his kingdom and his people, he became as an animal and lived in the wild.

This shakeup was necessary. It's what caused the King to humble himself and when he did, his sanity was restored. He cried out to God, repented and got his heart right. God not only restored him but he blessed him with bigger and better than what he had before.

Unfortunately, many people such as the King have to fall off a cliff before they humble themselves and get right with God. That was the case for me. I had to lose it all before I truly humbled myself before God and surrendered all.

Our loving and patient Lord tries to rescue us before we harm ourselves. But having a prideful heart keeps you from recognizing and dealing with the pride in yourself. It prevents you from being sensitive to the Holy Spirit's quick conviction. It blocks you from receiving the warnings. It causes you to justify your actions instead of being repentant. Don't allow pride to deceive you.

"Before a downfall the heart is haughty, but humility comes before honor." -Proverbs 18:4

God had to go deep and uproot this dangerous tree from my life. The tree of pride makes up of many branches, here is a list of some:

Pray that God will place the mirror of his truth in front of you as you read these signs of pride in a person's life.

- Arrogance, believing you are superior to others (Judgmental attitude)
- Self-centeredness
- Unwillingness to recognize/admit personal flaws
- Justify your actions/unwillingness to apologize
- Unforgiveness
- Be judgmental
- Reluctance to serve
- Boasting
- Envy
- Refusing advice/unteachable
- Get irritated when someone tries to teach them something
- Seeking Recognition
- Ingratitude
- Self-righteousness
- Rebel against God or God-ordained spiritual leaders
- Lack submission to authority
- Quick to speak, but slow to actively listen
- Constantly talking over someone else as they speak
- Defensiveness
- Controlling
- Manipulate others

- Obsession with appearance
- Flaunt your figure
- Spend a lot of time on your appearance

It's important to remember that **you are not immune** to experiencing moments of pride. However, being aware of these signs will help you reflect on your attitudes and behaviors which will lead to quick repentance.

After you allow God to do the uprooting, there is still the daily act of maintenance. The common belief is that you have to feel convicted of sin in order to repent, but we can't trust our feelings. The scripture tells us,

> "The heart is deceitful above all things, and desperately sick; who can understand it?" -Jeremiah 17:9

Make a daily habit of repenting whether you feel the urge to or not. This keeps your heart right.

This is part of my personal prayer each morning:

> "Lord, I repent of pride and any selfish motives. Show me any way in me that doesn't please you. Purify my heart from all unrighteousness."

The deadly sin of pride will prevent you from surrendering all to Christ.

It keeps believers blinded and deceived into thinking that they're good enough. That is why asking God to search our hearts and show us anything that is separating us from him, is so important. You do not want anything to prevent you from having an intimate love relationship with Jesus.

THE TRUST FACTOR

I can tell you friends, there is a difference from being a "good" Christian and living fully surrendered. It is literally two different lives. When God called me to surrender, I wasn't living in compromise or rebellion.

In fact, I led a moral, godly life, many other believers looked up to me and my faith. I was convinced that I loved Jesus. I was committed to a spirit-filled church and even led ministry groups. **I didn't go from dark to light, I went from light to pure light.**

God is all about our heart. Looking good on paper impresses people but it doesn't impress him. You can look and act good your entire life and still not be right with God and fulfilling your true purpose.

Surrender is not a dirty word. There is so much resistance to the idea of surrender for different reasons. To start out, our human flesh nature wants our way. We love our comforts and we want things to make sense to us. That is why so many follow the culture instead of the Bible. **Everyone's a Christian until it gets biblical.**

But I believe it all comes down to one reason and that is a lack of trust in God. Many Christians don't really trust the one that is asking them for everything. They don't know Jesus like that.

It's like having an acquaintance ask you if they could move into your house for a month. You'd be like, um nope. I don't really know you. You wouldn't give up your comforts and you wouldn't trust a stranger with complete access to your property, right?

Now it would be different if your best friend had the same request. Even if you hesitated, you would probably agree to them moving in for a month because you share a close relationship. You have history together, there's that love and trust. The trust factor is everything.

It's easier to let go and trust God when you believe beyond a shadow of a doubt that he loves you and he is for you. But if you don't have that close, intimate relationship with God or if you blame him for your trauma, then you won't fully trust him. Many have believed the lie that if they give God everything then he will somehow fail them.

The problem is, many doubt the fact that **God is good.**

This is the same old lie that the devil has pushed since the beginning of time. The very first humans ever created believed this lie and we are suffering the consequences of their actions now because of it. Adam and Eve lived a perfect existence in the Garden of Eden. God gave them access to everything. Everything except one forbidden fruit tree. He warned them to not eat of the tree or they would die.

But the craftiest of all, the serpent, said to the woman, "Did God really say, 'You must not eat from any tree in the garden'?" Eve told him of God's warning. But the serpent said, "You will certainly not die. For God knows that when you eat from it your eyes will be opened, and you will be like God, knowing good and evil."

The enemy deceived Adam and Eve into disobeying God and so they were cursed and we are still living under that curse of sin today. Read Genesis chapters 2-3 to learn more.

Just imagine how different everything would be now if Adam and Eve trusted God's character and rebuked the serpent. But instead, the enemy was able to convince Eve that God was not trustworthy. She was deceived into believing that God wasn't really that good. That he was holding out on her, holding back his best.

The enemy hasn't changed.

He has far too many believers convinced of this same lie. It's the lie that tells us, surrender equals misery. But the truth sets us free! And the truth is, the surrendered life comes with greater rewards. Rewards that you cannot put a price tag on. When you give God your all, he gives you back much more than you could ever imagine.

I have never had more peace, favor and protection than when I chose to surrender all to Jesus Christ.

Everything changes when you reject the lies of the enemy and accept the truth. The truth is God's ways are so much better than yours, his timing really is perfect, his character is flawless and he will never fail you. You can take that to the bank.

If you are struggling with trusting God you may need to stop and reflect on his perfect track record. You might start smiling as you look back at how good God has been in your life. Thank God for his faithfulness. There are times that he has protected you, provided and healed you without you even knowing.

To give you a clear understanding of what **true surrender** looks like:

>Lord, I give you my **relationships.**
>
>Lord, I give you my **family.**
>
>Lord, I give you my **hurt.**
>
>Lord, I give you my **expectations.**
>
>I give you my **finances.**
>
>I give you my **entertainment.**
>
>I give you my **time.**
>
>I give you my **plans.**
>
>I give you my **past.**
>
>I give you my **sin.**
>
>I give you my **future.**
>
>I give you my **whole heart.**

Whatever you want to do in me Lord, I'm yours.

One of the most sobering passages in the Bible is in Matthew 7: discerning who is a true and false disciple.

"Not everyone who says to me, 'Lord, Lord,' will enter the kingdom of heaven, but only the one who does the will of my Father who is in heaven. Many will say to me on that day, 'Lord, Lord, did we not prophesy in your name and in your name drive out demons and in your name perform many miracles? Then I will tell them plainly, 'I never knew you. Away from me, you evildoers!' I will know that you are my true disciple, by your fruit."

That is a hard truth right! God does not care about performance apart from surrender. Surrendering all is the foundation for godly fruit. It's the key to becoming a true disciple. Until you take this step than you will not be living the full life of freedom and purpose that God has planned for you.

I hear many believers say that they trust God. But does *God trust you?*

God is looking for the ones that will surrender all, have a pure heart and obey no matter the cost. Then he can trust you with greater kingdom assignments. You have been tested and now he knows that you will get the job done right. He knows that you will complete the task all for his glory, not yours. It is amazing when God promotes you to a whole new level of open doors, favor and influence because he trusts you.

Surrendering all is giving God the canvas so that he can paint a masterpiece. You are that masterpiece.

Call to action:
I encourage you friends to soul search and ask God to heal you and correct any misconceptions that you may be believing. Humbly confess and repent for unforgiveness, pride, addictions, idols, selfish motives, fear, doubt, word curses spoken and anything else that he brings to your mind. Allow him to go deep and do the work.

Surrender all to your loving, faithful and righteous heavenly Father. Watch him amaze you in ways that you never could have imagined. If you have chosen to surrender all, *your best is yet to come!*

CHAPTER 5

CRAZY FAITH

Let me start out by saying that it's only by the grace of God that I'm still believing and enduring what you will read in this next chapter.

For most, my past is relatable. Every other person that I've talked to has been devastated by addiction, abandonment or divorce. Unfortunately, it's all too common.

But what most find hard to believe is the mind-blowing promises from God of what's to come. On this long journey of over ten years and in the midst of great adversity, I still wait and trust God with expectation.

This is the part of my book where you might need to buckle your seat belt cause it's all so wild!

So, I'm sure you are wondering, what are the promises? Here are two of the big ones that I am believing God to fulfill.

PROMISES OF GOD

- God has spoken that, "Robert will have a Saul to Paul encounter, a night to day difference and he will never be the same." I have not even spoken to Robert in over a decade, yet God has repeatedly told me that he will reconcile, redeem and restore us. God also made it clear that he's intentionally "waiting for it to be dead in order to resurrect it."

Another 'only God could do it' word is about having children. As I explained earlier, growing up I did not have the desire to be a mother. But in my twenties, God rebuked me for speaking against it; I repented and have since surrendered to God's perfect will for my life. He has placed his desires in my heart.

- God shook me when he declared, "I come against those who have spoken infertility over you! That is a lie. You will have Elijahs and Elishas come out of your womb."

I know this all sounds crazy! It seems Foolish. Illogical. Dead. Impossible. How do I still believe? I stay laser-focused looking through the **LENS OF FAITH**.

The same wonder working God that parted the Red Sea, gave Abraham a biological child at 100 years old and reconciled Gomer to Hosea, is the same God today. He hasn't lost his power. He hasn't stopped performing miracles. He still resurrects dead things. He still keeps all of his promises.

"Jesus Christ is the same yesterday, today and forever." -Hebrews 13:8

Do you believe he is?

DIVINE CONFIRMATIONS

Along with God's gift of supernatural grace and his perspective every single day, he also continues to give me on going confirmations. God speaks to us through different sources such as when reading the Bible, during prayer, through the Holy Spirit, divine appointments, dreams, visions and prophecy.

In my case, I believe he has used prophecy so much because he knew that I would talk myself out of all of this but I wouldn't be able to deny all the messengers that he sends.

As I'm sitting at my desk typing that sentence, I feel the power of the Holy Spirit hit me and I have to take a praise break. Insert crying emoji. God is so real and intentional!

As of today, I have recorded over 70 clear prophetic confirmations regarding my future and some have already come to pass.

Usually, it is complete strangers that approach me who may not even know my first name, yet they know intimate details of my life. In fact, some may have been angels in disguise because at times these messengers have come up to me to deliver a powerful word from the

Lord then immediately walk away. No small talk. Then when I turn around, they're gone and I never see them again.

> "Do not forget to show hospitality to strangers, for by doing so some people have shown kindness to angels without knowing it." -Hebrews 13:2

Another sign is the unnatural response that occurs when God is speaking through someone to me. Most often, when I'm receiving a word that's truly from the Lord, the fire of the Holy Spirit falls on me and I suddenly become overwhelmed with emotion. That's one way to tell if it's a good word vs. a God word. There have been times when suddenly the power of God confirms in my spirit what is being said, and I fall forward while weeping uncontrollably. This is not a natural response. It is a supernatural moment when heaven meets earth.

There are amazing ways that God has confirmed his promises to me, really too many to count, but I will share a few of my favorite encounters with you that really stand out.

THE RIGHT MAN

It's the weekend, just four months after my husband walked out and I'm visiting my family in California. We planned a road trip and rented a house for a few days to attend a Christian conference. I was depressed and in survival mode after my marriage fell apart. So, when we arrived to the conference, I went to sit in the very back row where I could hide from the crowd.

As thousands of attendees are in this packed low-lit arena worshipping, suddenly, a college aged man who is standing by my side turns to me. He bursts out saying, "Your husband is the right man for you and God has a specific plan for his life. He's the best husband for you." Then he goes right back into worship like nothing ever happened.

It was such a surreal moment that I questioned if it was just my imagination, but my sister who was on the other side of me overheard every word! She says, "Wow only God!" then she repeated word for word what I also heard. This boosted our faith in that moment. God made sure that I had an eye witness to keep me from doubting. He is so intentional.

Another example of an unforgettable encounter is the promise from God that I will birth children one day.

ELIJAHS AND ELISHAS

It's Thursday night and I have dinner plans with my friend, Lauri. As I'm driving, I ask her if we could swing by my sister's church real quick to pick up some new mascara that I accidently left in her car. My sister was leading worship at a women's conference that night and told me to stop by and pick it up on our way to go eat.

When we arrived at the church, we both quietly sat away from the crowd in the low-lit sanctuary so we would not be a distraction. The speaker suddenly shouts out, "God has me here for one person." My immediate thought was, how nice that one of these women will be encouraged.

I'm just here to pick something up and go is what I thought but God had totally different plans.

After a few minutes, I suddenly felt that we were supposed to stay at the conference and skip our dinner date. Except, I was sure my friend would disagree and we would head out soon. But why not just ask. So, I turn around to mention it but before I could say anything, she says, "I think we should stay here."

So here we are, all locked in listening to the speaker and the good word being preached. As she wraps up her message, she has us all stand up, eyes closed to worship and soak in God's presence.

My friend and I stood worshiping with a church full of women as the song, "Oh how he loves us" was blaring through the speakers. Our eyes are closed when all of a sudden, I could hear footsteps rushing in my direction. She comes right over to me and starts shouting over the loud music into my ear. With authority she says, "You're the one that God sent me for!"

Then she puts her hand on my belly and starts prophesying, "I come against those who have spoken infertility over you! That is a lie. You will have Elijahs and Elishas come out of your womb."

All of a sudden, I felt the power of God hit my body, head to toe fire, as I bowled over while weeping uncontrollably. I knew that this was a true word from the Lord because that type of physical reaction had never happened to me before. And for me to have that kind of powerful response to something that I didn't even desire or pray for, could only be supernatural.

On the other hand, my friend standing right next to me had been praying and trying for years to get pregnant. In fact, she was carrying major disappointment because her and her husband were unable to conceive. But that night, she also got prophesied that she would deliver babies. Promise fulfilled: Lauri now has three children.

This same woman that prophesied over us, was connected to my sister but only knew me by face. She comes up to me after the service that night and says, "God gave me a vision of you seven years ago but he said it wasn't time to tell you. But before you walked in here tonight, he told me you were coming and that now is the time to deliver this message to you. The vision I had, was of you at God's throne, he keeps trying to give you a child but you keep rejecting his wonderful gift. God says, Don't reject what I have for you."

I come in agreement with everything God has for my life. No more and no less.

What a night! We left that church on cloud nine, completely energized and amazed by the power of God. When I returned home that night, I reflected on all the details of what had just happened. I thought, Wow, I wasn't even supposed to be there! I was just going to pick up my mascara and leave.

It was a *divine setup*.

God started showing me that it was actually all him. He set up every detail. It wasn't an accident that I forgot that mascara in the car. He used that mascara to get us where we needed to be in that moment.

To think that our God is so creative and strategic and he will use anything to accomplish his purposes. He used something as small as makeup to deliver something so grand. If you like surprises, follow Jesus for non-stop creative surprises in your life.

This next event is another example of God displaying his amazing power like only he can.

MY BABY LEAPT

One day out of the blue, a woman named Irina, who is an acquaintance, asked me out to eat. She tells me, "I want to hear your story." Because I pray for divine appointments every day, I'm always expectant knowing that God has a purpose for every meet up. We decided to meet at a local salad spot. As soon as we arrived, we saw that it was a busy and noisy lunch hour, so we got a table in the corner.

At the time, Irina was pregnant with her first child. As we sat down to eat, she cuts to the chase and asks me to share the reason that I moved across the country and why I'm single.

So I began sharing my story, just as I have countless times before. As I'm giving her the details, her lack of emotion seemed odd to me. Usually, the person on the other end is very expressive but Irina was dead silent with no response, not even a raised eyebrow!

So, I just continued to share and as soon as I got to the part, "God told me I'm going to have Elijahs and Elijahs come out of my womb." All of a sudden, Irina jumped up out of her chair and stood there with tears in her eyes. I was like, whoa what just happened!?

She tells me, "I am five months pregnant but I have not felt my baby move in five days. I have been praying that I would feel him move. And as soon as you said, Elijahs and Elishas would come out of your womb; my baby leapt in my belly! Then when you stopped, my baby stopped moving."

We were both shook and emotional as we felt the power and presence of God right there in that busy restaurant. It was a moment I will never forget. After we said goodbye, I was driving back home just stunned and the Holy Spirit says,

"Every promise I have given you will come to pass, even the ones you don't care about."

I'm reminded of Elizabeth in the Bible, who was pregnant at a ripe age with John the Baptist. Her baby leapt as soon as she saw Mary who was also pregnant, with Jesus. (Luke 1:41)

I get emotional as I go down memory lane to write down these amazing events. It is supernatural God encounters like these that have helped me hold on to his promises with unwavering confidence, even in the face of fierce opposition. God constantly assures me that he will do just as he says and his encouragement is always timely. He sends just the right person at just the right time to say just the right thing.

I'm reminded of another amazing God encounter. This is for my ladies (men can skip this part). When I was a teen, all the girls in school were starting their period at the same time at around fifteen-sixteen years old. My dad had a strict rule in our home that we couldn't wear makeup or get our ears pierced until we did. So naturally, me being the oldest of my six sisters, I expected to start first. But no, it was my sister who is a year younger than me that started first and then her body suddenly blossomed. I was upset by this and bullied at school by all the popular girls because I was the only one that didn't transition from a girl to a woman. In fact, it didn't happen for me until like a year or so later.

Fast forward to me now as an adult, I almost forgot about this distant childhood memory until a few years ago when God reminded me. He takes me in a time capsule all the way back to that time as a teenager and says, "Even you starting your period later, I did that. I knew you would be a mother later. I'm preserving you. Your body will not be your age when you have children."

Wow right. God literally sets things up even when we are children for the fulfillment of our destiny later in life. Nothing is an accident or a coincidence. As I write this now, I am forty-eight years old, but his promise still stands. I will give birth to "Elijahs and Elishas" (men of God, prophets). This is no hard task for the God who spoke all of creation into existence.

Last year, God encouraged me with a testimony told by a Pastor visiting from India. I knew this story was meant for me to hear and remember. He shared that this woman in his town really wanted to have a child but she had no ovaries. Still, his church prayed over her and they all believed for a miracle. Well guess what! God touched her body, then she naturally got pregnant and had a healthy child. Without ovaries! How do you explain that?

Don't tell me he can't do it. We need to stop putting limits on the Almighty. He doesn't fit in our narrow sighted, rational box. Either he's God or he's not.

COAST TO COAST

I am always amazed at how our great God is so detailed and so strategic. He moves in such a way to prove that he does what no man can do. Like how he sends me messengers at different ends of the nation to deliver the same word.

For example, there have been times that I've been invited to a local church that I've never heard of for an event. As I'm there, a complete stranger makes a beeline towards me, they're on a mission to deliver a word from God. The prophecy is spot on and confirms exactly what I'm believing God for.

Then a short time later, I take a trip to the opposite side of the country. As I'm here visiting family, I once again get invited to visit a "random" local church.

As I'm there, another stranger targets me and confirms the exact same word. The exact same word that the last person all the way on the other end of the country just spoke over me! How do you naturally explain this!? You simply cannot. It is really proof of God.

Like the Friday that I visited a church where a young woman comes up from behind me and asks me, "Do you have children?" I gave her a confused look and said, "No." Then she says, "You will be a great mother. Not only to your own children but to others around you, you will be a nurturing mother figure." She just dropped that confirmation and left. I turn around to spot her but she's gone. I never saw her again; it could have been an angelic visitation. Then I'm flying back across the country and when I return home, it's the same scenario. Another complete stranger delivers a powerful word that confirms the one before.

God has set up this supernatural cross country ping pong match just so he can wow me and boost my faith, which he never stops doing.

Watching God move like this gives me the faith boost that I need to stay faithful to his plan and purposes no matter what. He means to keep me steadfast and to energize my hope by doing what only he can do. He alone gets all the glory!

"I am the Lord, the God of all mankind. Is anything too hard for me?" -Jeremiah 32:27

"What is impossible with men is possible with God." -Luke 18:27

Even if you are someone that does not believe in the prophetic or that God still speaks today, how do you explain the enormous amount of accurate ongoing words of knowledge from complete strangers? Over 70! These downloads are either written down or audio recorded. There have been times that God has me go back and read or listen to remind myself of my future, to give me fresh hope and come in agreement with him. Whether it's through the prophetic words, dreams, visions or the peace, God is constantly reminding me to stay laser focused on him.

I want to mention an important point, so many people focus on the prophetic aspect of my story and yes wow all those divine encounters are so amazing! I also have shared my story with people who are unfamiliar or doubt the prophetic. I am not solely believing and enduring because I have all these direct messages from God, spoken through others. I also press in with the Lord every day. Listening improves discernment. The more you listen to God, the better you can distinguish his voice from other sounds in your minds.

I know his voice because I take the time to listen. It is undistracted, quiet, quality time that we need to discern the truth. Having a tight relationship with Jesus, means you won't just come to him with a wish list. You also welcome his warnings, his conviction and his discipline. It goes back to the, "whatever you want Lord. Here I am" heart posture.

Time and time again God has confirmed and continues to confirm, that I am on the right track. But the reality is, the promises that I'm believing for, well most will have to see it to really believe it. That's usually the way it goes in a world that lacks God's eternal heavenly perspective.

No one in their right mind would still be holding on but I'm not in *my* right mind, I'm in *God's mind*.

WORTH THE WAIT

Meanwhile, in this time of preparation, it's a surrender of my will every day. I want God to do whatever he needs to do in and through me. Of course, that doesn't mean it's been easy. I have hard days and there have been times that God has to remind me that he is true. I remember this particular time, that I had to be put in check.

To give you an understanding, I make it a point to keep strict boundaries with men. I don't play around; that means no dating. I also don't collect guy friends to pretend date. If you know what I mean. It's a slippery slope. I know how sneaky the devil is. He really is a sneaky snake who plays on what we want.

That being said, I've had bachelors pursue me as well as marriage proposals by men who have watched me from a distance. I have never been tempted except for this one time. Several years ago, I met a guy at a church group who I wasn't attracted to but he flattered me. He flirted hard. He knew exactly what to say and I took the bait. We never got physical or anything, but still we would text each other late at night.

One night after a few weeks of texting each other, the Lord rebuked me and said, "Don't cheat on your promises!"

Wow right. Don't cheat on your promises! Well, that was the end of that and I never spoke to him again. It's as if God was telling me, I didn't bring you this far to let you get caught up in a moment of weakness. Snap out of it!

Of course, I want to date, to go on adventures and all the things but I want to obey God more. The fear of God really does keep us protected. God is more invested in our story than we are. He's had grand plans for you before you even learned to walk. He is for you not against you. God's love for you is beyond comparison.

> "Before I shaped you in the womb, I knew you intimately. I had divine plans for you before I gave you life." -Jeremiah 1:5

Remember, God is outside of our time. We focus on age and calendars but God dwells in a different realm - the spirit realm - which is beyond the perception of our physical senses. It's not that God isn't real; it's a matter of his not being limited by the physical laws and dimensions that govern our world. He's not on our clock. Moses used a simple yet profound analogy in describing the timelessness of God:

> "For a thousand years in Your sight are like a day that has just gone by, or like a watch in the night."
> -Psalm 90:4

"The Lord is not slow in keeping his promises, as some understand slowness. He has patience for everyone involved." -2 Peter 3:9

I know that we as a culture hate waiting for anything. We are part of an impatient society that chases after instant gratification. While technology can be positive, it also has made us impatient. We live in a world of touch and go but God is not a touch and go God. In fact, often times he's just the opposite.

We are a microwave generation, but God is a crockpot God. A microwave cooks quickly but often produces unhealthy food, while a crockpot takes hours but yields much better results. If you've had a meal cooked from a crockpot then you know what I'm talking about. It's worth the wait.

Some of the reasons that we don't like to wait can be that we want to know what the future holds; it makes us feel more in control. Waiting can give us FOMO (fear of missing out). We imagine that we will be happier once the wait is over. Really, it's thinking that we know better than God. God is interested more in the journey, than the destination. We are usually focused on the end goal but he cares more about the process.

Many see waiting as a wilderness or desert season. It's put in a negative context, as if we're just waiting for a better life. When in fact, it should be one of the most fruitful times in our lives. God wants to grow an orchard in your desert, one that bears much rich fruit that will impact others.

"See, I am doing a new thing! Now it springs up; do you not perceive it? I am making a way in the wilderness and streams in the wasteland." -Isaiah 43:19

We need to recognize why God calls us to wait. He does it for his glory and to make us more like Jesus, whose whole life could be called a waiting game. He waited for his disciples, he waited for the crowds, he waited for his parents, he waited for crucifixion, he waited for glorification, and he is waiting to return. His life, death, and resurrection are pictures of faithful waiting.

He is our example when waiting seems so horribly hard and contentment feels just out of reach. When God has us waiting, it's not because he wants to hold back his best or to make us miserable. He is always very intentional just like God the Father is with Jesus. He sees the bigger, better picture.

I wouldn't be who I am today if it weren't for the isolation, purging, refining, testing and pressing in. It's in the wait that God restores and aligns our heart. He is in the waiting. It's in the wait that he molds our character and cultivates intimacy and dependency on Him alone. Seek his face, not his hand. He is the prize. He is the end goal.

"Remember, God is outside of our time. We focus on age and calendars but God dwells in a different realm - the spirit realm - which is beyond the perception of our physical senses. It's not that God isn't real; it's a matter of his not being limited by the physical laws and dimensions that govern our world. He's not on our clock."

"We are a microwave generation, but God is a *crockpot God.*"

CHAPTER 6

GOD'S PERSPECTIVE

I get asked if Robert and I talk or if I keep up with him; the answer is no. I have not stayed in contact with him or anyone associated with him since 2013. But still, there have been a few times that I have been given bad news about him.

Like that one day, a year after our separation when I got a surprise direct message in my inbox. It was from a girl that he was dating who not only looked me up online, but she went as far as creating a fake account just so she could talk to me undetected. She asked me to call her, and as soon as I did, she began venting. She was upset about Robert's mental state and his worsening spiral into addiction. She also claimed to be pregnant and said that he wouldn't return her calls. She was asking me for advice but she also wanted to make sure that I didn't want him back because all he did was talk about me.

I really didn't know what to say at the time, but hearing this felt like a punch to the gut. After I hung up the phone, I called a woman of prayer who has spoken into my life and asked to see her right away.

When I arrived at her house, I told her what happened and as tears flowed down my face, I shouted, "It's not that I don't believe that God can do the miracles. I believe he can do it. But if this is true, I don't want it!" Her response was, "Let's worship."

As I'm sitting on her couch and we began to worship, she starts praying over me, "God has not forgotten your faithfulness. He is going to bless every single moment that you have been faithful." After that night of worshipping God in the midst of confusion and disappointment, he gave me such peace. I didn't give up that day. I've wrestled with doubt on this long journey but hope always wins. I later found out that girl lied about being pregnant; they broke up and she married a different man.

Receiving news about Robert in his rebellion, is hard and seems contradictory to what God has said will happen. The enemy has even used information to set me back at times. His goal is to discourage, get me to doubt and to give up all together. But God won't allow it.

In moments of discouragement, I have questioned God's plan, "Why do you want me to be with this man? You can send me a better man to marry and you will still get the glory."

Some of God's responses are:

"I'm going to use you to display my wonders."

"I'm waiting for it to be dead so I can resurrect it, for my greater glory."

"Your testimony will lead people to salvation."

"Your obedience will save future generations."

These big statements sound amazing but they come at a high price. The cost is, "Whatever you want, Lord. I'm yours."

If you agree to surrender your will to God's will, he'll lead you through a difficult but beautiful process of transformation. It's the refining fire that's necessary to burn off everything that doesn't resemble him. This process purifies and produces something far more valuable than gold – Christlike character. And when you come out of the fire, you won't even smell like smoke. That's the redeeming God we serve.

"I have refined you, though not as silver; I have tested you in the furnace of affliction." -Isaiah 48:10

I remember one day watching a woman prune her rose bushes. As she was cutting off what was dead, to my surprise she also trimmed off the pretty blooms and branches, all the way to the ground.

It made me think, "that stump is going to die, why would she cut what's green, she cut too far back." A few months later, those same bushes grew back healthier, full of vibrant color and more fragrant than before. Then the Holy Spirit tells me that he is that Gardner, "That's what I'm doing in your life. I'm doing a new thing."

You see, you may think you are healthy or good enough because you have some green branches or a few pretty blooms. I mean, you're not dead right?! But our skilled Gardner God knows how much more vibrant you will be if you let him do the pruning. Of course, none of us like the uncomfortable pruning and refining process. But in order to have a beautiful life, he needs to get down to the root. The master Gardner is uprooting, removing rot, cutting off what's unnecessary, watering with his love and replacing old soil with new life-changing miracle grow.

My friend of twenty years once told me, "Leah, what would have crushed anyone has crushed forth out of you, a beautiful fragrance." That's the result of God's pruning power. We read in John 15 the importance of pruning/refining.

"I am the true vine, and my Father is the gardener. He cuts off every branch in me that bears no fruit, while every branch that does bear fruit, he prunes so that it will be even more fruitful. I am the vine; you are the branches. If you remain in me and I in you, you will bear much fruit; apart from me you can do nothing. This is to my Father's glory, that you bear much fruit, showing yourselves to be my disciples."

I encourage you to allow our loving Lord to do his work until he is done. Don't Give Up. It's worth it! When God is calling you to go against all logic, it's important to have his perspective. Also known as the, Lens of Faith. You see, we get so caught up in our timelines, our feelings, our past, our plans, our limited vision and our logic. But when we ask for his perspective, we gain his understanding. God shows us glimpses of the greater picture. He reminds us that it's not about us. We have a role to play in a much bigger storyline.

Jesus Christ is King. The creator of heaven and earth. He is the Alpha and Omega, the beginning and the end. He knows our first day from our last and all the details in between. God wrote your story before you were born. He is very purposeful in all he does and his timing is perfect. If you are struggling and you need fresh hope, ask God to give you his perspective and a greater understanding of your situation. He will do it!

DEATH TO LIFE

When God first let me know it's time to start writing this book, three years ago, I was full of excitement and the chapters began to flow out of me. But after the enemy used circumstances and family members to deeply discourage me, I took a break from writing. Along with that, I know that authors usually wait to write their tell-all testimony once they are on the other side of victory and time has passed. Going on single lunch dates and sharing is one thing but publicly telling the world as I still wait is next level.

In addition, is knowing that I'm supposed to share the hard details, instead of being safe and vague in my storytelling. God really is my editor, and he made it clear that so many more people will be able to relate by my being transparent and real, which is who I have always been – an open book. Being relatable will bring greater impact and deliverance to many.

"But God everything seems so dead to the point of decomposing now" I tell him.

He brings me back to his word, "I am actually waiting for it all to be dead, so that I can resurrect it." God often encourages me with the amazing Bible story of Lazarus. It reminds me that this is not his first rodeo.

Lazarus was one of Jesus's few real friends and he loved him. In fact, the only time Jesus wept in the Bible was when Lazarus died. But Jesus could have prevented his death. He healed people all the time. His sisters,

Mary and Martha even sent word to Jesus to tell him that Lazarus was sick. But instead of rushing to his side, his response was,

"This sickness will not end in death. No, it is for God's glory so that God's Son may be glorified through it."

He left everyone super confused and upset. Then he intentionally delayed and waited two more days before he went back to check on Lazarus. I mean if you loved someone that was dying and could simply heal them, wouldn't you rush to their side asap?

But Jesus was in no hurry. Instead, he was more bothered by the disciples' lack of faith. When his disciples questioned him, Jesus response was, "For your sake, I am glad I was not there when Lazarus got sick, so that you may believe. Now let's go to him."

Jesus arrived back to the town where Lazarus was already dead for four days! He was deader than dead. Everyone was freaking out as they ran to Jesus but he was chill and unbothered. Mary was upset with Jesus, "Lord, if you had been here, my brother would not have died." When Jesus saw Martha whom he loved, weeping, the Bible says, Jesus was deeply moved in spirit and troubled by their sadness. Jesus then said, "take me to Lazarus's tomb," then Jesus wept. The Jews said,

"See how much he loved him."

"Could not he who opened the eyes of the blind have kept this man from dying?" others said.

Jesus ignores all the chatter. He tells Martha to remove the gravestone, she replies by telling him that there is too much odor since his dead body laid in the tomb for four days.

Then Jesus said, "Did I not tell you that if you believe, you will see the glory of God?"

(He really does not like when people lack faith and doubt him.) So, they removed the stone and Jesus prayed to his Father God for guidance, then he shouted, "Lazarus, come out!" The dead man came out, his hands and feet wrapped with strips of linen and a cloth around his face! Jesus said to them, "Take off the grave clothes and let him go," The people were all amazed and word of this miracle spread throughout the regions.

Factual accounts in history like these encourage and convict me. God is the same God today as he was way back then. He still baffles the logic of man. He still resurrects dead things.

"Walk by faith, not by sight."
-2 Corinthians 5:7

When I delayed in writing this book, God called me out on my faith. "Do you really believe that I will do exactly what I promised no matter how dead it seems? Will you obey me no matter what people think?" When God asks us to do the hardest things, he is asking us to trust him. Period. It is him that will do what seems impossible but he often wants to partner with us. Without trust it won't get done.

Duty is ours; the results are God's.

It hasn't been easy. I've had to allow God to rid me of any fear of man or people pleasing in order to write this book with exactly what he leads me to say, without holding back. God is asking me to take a leap of even greater faith and share the miracle while in the middle. Before it's "safe." Before it's said and done. Before the haters and doubters start supporting me.

I remember years ago while talking with a friend she shouts, "Leah, if the Bible was written today, there would be a chapter written about you. You are living a modern-day Bible story. Your incredible journey of faith and endurance is like the ones we talk about in churches and Bible studies."

What baffles me is, the same Christians who say that they believe in the Bible and all the astounding miracles that Jesus performed, are the same ones that can be quick to doubt when they come face to face with a modern-day Bible story.

My thought is, so you believe in Shadrach, Meshach and Abednego who were sent by a King to burn in a blazing furnace but instead not even a hair on their heads was singed and the son of God was seen with them in the fire. But you have trouble believing that God will reconcile a dead marriage and give children to a woman in her forties? These are my thoughts when I face seasoned believers who don't believe that God will do what he's promised in my situation.

Ask yourself:

Would you believe Noah if you were standing with the mocking crowds as he was building the ark with no sign of rain? How about Abraham, the Bible says, "he was pretty much dead", as he waited for God to give him a son at 100 years old? Take David who killed a giant with a small rock? Would you try and stop Queen Esther from going to the King in order to save a nation?

Having God's perspective changes everything. The Bible is full of accounts of ordinary men and women who partnered with God to display his signs and wonders and change their generation. You could be part of a modern-day Bible story.

The people that I can relate to most; are not living. Instead, they are the ones we read and teach about such as Abraham, Joseph, Moses, Queen Esther, Job, Noah, Lazarus and Hosea. It's these faith heroes that went before me who keep me steady and trusting God in this long journey. Their true-life stories give me understanding and his perspective as I keep the faith because with God ALL things are possible.

In Hebrews, there is the hall of faith chapter that recalls some of the great men and women who trusted God. Even when what God was asking them to do, seemed impossible. I know I like to point to Bible characters a lot but hey they have the best stories!

One of my favorites is Abraham. God called him and his wife, Sarah to a foreign land, then tells them that they will have a son but get this – Abraham's 100 years old! We read that Sarah was barren, and her husband was past age and "good as dead." That part always makes me laugh. Good as dead! But he still believed God.

"Against all hope, Abraham in hope believed in the promise that comes by faith and he became the father of many nations, just as it had been said to him, without weakening in his faith, he faced the fact that his body was as good as dead-since he was about 100 years old- and that Sarah's womb was also dead. Yet he did not waver through unbelief regarding the promise of God, but was strengthened in his faith and gave glory to God, being fully persuaded that God had power to do what he had promised. This is why 'it was credited to him as righteousness.' -Romans 4, Hebrews 11

"We serve the God who gives life to the dead and calls things that are not as though they were."
-Romans 4: 17-23

Sometimes, God's plan will require you to look foolish.

LORD, GIVE US FAITH LIKE ABRAHAM.

When I look at our current culture and the world around me, my story doesn't make any sense. But when I study the Bible and read true stories like Abraham's, my story makes perfect sense.

I remember one day feeling discouraged so I asked God to show me a specific verse in his word to give me hope. I heard him say, Numbers 23:19. My first thought was, Numbers? Who reads the book of Numbers?

Is there anything encouraging in that book? But when I looked the verse up it greatly encouraged me.

"God is not human, that he should lie, not a human being, that he should change his mind. Does he speak and then not act? Does he promise and not fulfill?"
-Numbers 23:19

This powerful truth is one of my favorite life verses. I declare it as a constant and valued reminder. The Holy Spirit is so sweet and he constantly reminds me that no matter how impossible God's promises seem or how long it takes to fulfill them, they are Yes and Amen. You can count on the God who always comes through. He watches over every word to perform it.

The Lord is faithful and he helps me press on. He will get the glory in my life. He hasn't brought me this far to not finish what he started.

The definition of Endurance is: The ability to defy all logic and reason, to willingly accept suffering and hardship when faced with adversity without giving up.

"You're living a modern-day Bible story."

LENS OF FAITH

CHAPTER 7

RADICAL OBEDIENCE

How do you feel when you hear the words, surrender, obedience, holiness, repentance, sacrifice? Do you cringe? We as humans are selfish by nature and we don't like the idea of discomfort. We fight for control, and our desire is to do things our way.

We have been deceived into believing that obedience equals misery when really surrendering to God's will is the definition of living your best life. Knowing how much God really loves you and is for you changes everything.

I always say, favor follows radical obedience. The rewards of going all in are greater than the sacrifice.

Yes, God asks us for our life but he gives us back a much better life. He asks us for our time but he redeems time. He asks us for our broken heart and then gives us back a healed heart. The return on investment is at an all-time high in the kingdom of God.

Favor takes you places that hustling can't. You don't have to beg God or worry if he'll come through, he just does. It's when you don't even have to ask for things from God because he is already moving on your behalf.

He opens doors that you didn't even have to knock on! He grants you with supernatural grace, protection and peace that passes all understanding.
You constantly sense his hand guiding every detail of your day because you have given him permission.

God's purpose for giving you favor is not to build your kingdom, it's to build his. Favor is necessary for you to complete your God ordained destiny! God's favor helps us endure the race he's called us to run. It sustains and encourages us in a season of tested faith.

"Lord, you bless the righteous; you surround them with your favor as with a shield." -Psalm 5:12

> "Favor follows *radical obedience.*"

CHOOSE A SIDE

People pleasing and fear of man will prevent you from living a life of radical obedience. When God says go, don't filter the task through man's opinion first. We all want to be liked by people and by God but the reality is, you must choose a side.

God dealt with me on this one day early on in my ministry. Here I was sitting at my computer when he downloaded a zinger for me to post on social media. It was a good one but I knew that this one liner would not be popular. So, I was thinking of a way to edit it, to make it easier to receive. In that very moment, the Holy Spirit stopped me and said,

> "You can either please God or man, not both. Choose today."

Yikes. I was stunned. I made my decision clear that day, "I choose you Lord." Then he continues by telling me, "Not everyone will like what you have to say but I will be well pleased. You will be my mouthpiece. Say it exactly how I tell you to say it. The spiritually asleep will wake up, the dead will rise by the words that come out of your mouth. You will break the spirit of suicide off of people just by the words that come out of your mouth and you won't even know it."

I know that part of God's mandate on my life is to teach others righteousness, to set the captives free and to be an example of faith. We are meant to walk in our God given authority! Chains are broken and people are set free by the power of Jesus Christ in us.

Radical obedience is not a popular message but God didn't create us to be popular, we are meant to be purposeful. True freedom comes when you live to please an audience of one. Let God's opinion be what matters most.

TO LOVE IS TO OBEY

I remember as a teenager, my dad would tell me to complete a chore but sometimes I would get distracted doing something else. So, he would ask me again to wash the dishes or clean the living room. Time had passed and I still didn't finish my chores, When I walked back in the room, I told my dad, I love you. He quickly responded, "Do you love me? Those are just nice words. If you love me, you'll obey me." Ouch.

Just like our earthly Father, our heavenly Father also requires our obedience.

Many claim to love God but obedience is proof that we really love him. Jesus repeatedly tells us in his word, "If you love me, you'll obey me." -John 14:15

Jesus doesn't tell us to do something that he hasn't done himself. He knows the cost of obedience because he paid the ultimate price. Even though he was a perfect man without sin, he obeyed his Father by going to the bloody cross to sacrifice his life for our sins.

Imagine spending your entire life healing the sick, raising the dead, performing miracles and ministering to the same people that would send you to your death. Jesus even died for those that hated him. There is no greater love, no greater sacrifice than what Jesus did at calvary. If Jesus can sacrifice his life, then we can sacrifice our plans, our timeline, our relationships and our selfish desires, right? He alone deserves our all.

God requires our unconditional obedience. He doesn't say, Obey me if it makes sense, Obey me if you are comfortable doing so, Obey me if others support you. Obey me if I don't make you wait too long. There are no conditions. God simply says, "Trust and obey me." God is well pleased when we say, Yes, no matter the cost.

Our Creator is so great that he spoke the universe into existence yet so detailed that he designed the body of a tiny insect. Do you really expect him to perform like us mere mortals? He tells us what to expect with this verse.

"As the heavens are higher than the earth, so are my ways higher than your ways and my thoughts than your thoughts." -Isaiah 55:99

Meaning, he doesn't perform like we do. If everything you do is somewhat comfortable and logical than you might want to question if you're really living surrendered. I have watched many believers do what they want to do as they put God on it. They will try and convince others that everything they choose to do is "God's will" when really, they are doing what they want to do. The truth is that many are driven by selfish motives.

Your flesh will fight having to wait. Having to give up comforts. Having to hear the opinion of man. Walking by faith is not always easy. However, the heart posture of surrendering all is, Lord your will be done, not mine.

The same God of Moses, Noah, Queen Esther, Abraham, Sarah and Joseph asks us to trust him completely. If we do, he will blow our minds. He will show up and show out like no man ever could.

The Red Sea never parted until Moses. An ark was never built before Noah. No other queen risked her life like Esther. It was Abraham who had a son at 100 years old. It was Joseph that went from a pit to a prison to a palace.

God wants to partner with us in order to display his wonders but this takes radical obedience from a place of surrender. When we submit to the process, it's then that he can trust us with more. He wants to promote us to advance the kingdom. That is the great commission.

> "God didn't create you to be popular, you are meant to be *purposeful.*"

KNOWING GOD'S WILL

God is not the author of confusion. God doesn't want confused, frustrated Christians wandering around anxiously searching for purpose. He wants people who are living confidently and peacefully in His will.

There are ways to be sure that you're in that heavenly alignment.

One of the main indicators is Peace. When you surrender all and are walking in God's will, then supernatural peace always follows. It's the confirmation you need for every decision. It's a peace that passes all understanding, like the Bible says. Meaning it doesn't make natural sense.

In my case, when I hit rock bottom, God relocated me far from any loved ones, to a different culture and land and kept me isolated while he performed heart surgery. He stripped me of my comforts and all that was familiar. But even then, I had unexplainable peace.

Now the opposite is also true. You'll know that you're not in God's will by the lack of peace. Anytime you feel stress, anxiety or stiving take over in any situation, stop and check yourself. We can get ourselves in bad situations when we are led by the flesh instead of the spirit. Whenever I am striving, trying to make something happen, or am not obeying God, such as repenting for sin, there is no peace and that's always a clear indicator.

The devil can only imitate, he cannot originate. He's never original. All he does is counterfeit and deceive. But he cannot counterfeit the Peace that only God provides.

Another way to know that you're in God's will is Provision. God never orders something he doesn't pay for. When he gives you an assignment, he partners with you, he leads you and always provides what you need to complete the task at hand. After all, it's his ask.

Favor follows radical obedience. You can trust and expect him to always make a way even when there seems to be no way. There have been countless times that God has proven to be my provider. You can count on him.

Another example of his favor is in Preservation. The enemy will try and have you believe the lies that you're "wasting time", "you're getting too old" or "it's too late." But the truth is God preserves the faithful. I get asked what my anti-aging secret is since most people think I'm much younger than I am. My running joke is it's "Jesus serum". But really, It's statistically proven that the people who spend time daily meditating on God's word, age differently. It's that peace. People who constantly worry, look worried. Which makes sense because the enemy wants to cause you to worry and stress. He is here to destroy but God came to give life and life to the fullest.

You cannot worry and trust God at the same time.

These triple P's are signs that you are in God's will.
Peace. Provision. Preservation.

Jesus gives peace amid every storm. The devil creates storms that rob you of your peace. But it's not just physical preservation, God will preserve what concerns you. You will not regret the time you've spent as a faithful and obedient servant of our worthy King Jesus.

He is our Peace. Our Provider. Our Preserver.

"The righteous will never be shaken; they will be remembered forever. They will have no fear of bad news; because their hearts are steadfast, trusting in the Lord." -Psalm 112: 6-7

Pause and take a praise break as you reflect on God's goodness and faithfulness.

> "O love the Lord, all you His godly ones!
> The Lord preserves the faithful." -Psalm 31:23

Step out and trust God with whatever he is asking of you. His mercies are new every morning. His grace will be sufficient to stay the course. But you must stay focused and keep close to him every day, through his word, prayer, praise, worship and building community with fellow faith filled believers in your local church.

> "God never *orders* something that he doesn't *pay for.*"

STAY FOCUSED

It is not easy to walk away from the common and popular pursuit of the "American dream". They might not say it out loud, but most people have greater respect for those that are married, have kids and are chasing after the world's success. When your choices go against all the norms, it messes with people's heads. They want your life to fit the average mold. Their mold.

I believe if you are living a life of radical obedience, you cannot depend on others to cheer you on. Very few will truly understand. We must learn to encourage ourselves in the Lord.

God has sent me faith filled saints that stand with me, continue to pray and encourage me but at this point many do not. The attacks of the enemy have been fierce. The devil knows how relational I am so he tries to use people to try and get me off track. I have been doubted, slandered, mocked and rejected for my radical obedience to God's call on my life.

There have even been a couple female ministers who know my story and who say that "God keeps his promises" yet those same ones have tried to set me up on dates with other men.

It can feel discouraging to have fellow Christians detach when you need support the most. Especially when the hostility is coming from those closest to you. They say, the strongest opposition usually comes from relatives and that's been my experience. I have been told by doubting family members that, "God didn't confirm any of this to them" or "Robert has free will".

It's true that God has given us all free will but he is also Sovereign. God's plan for people takes into account their free will. My challenge is this, why would God promise you something even while knowing that someone's free will would change your outcome? Does God play games? Does he trick? Does he cause confusion? As if God didn't know someone's future choices before he made those promises to you. When I face opposition brought on by people, God points me to this Bible truth,

> "What if others do not have faith? Will their lack of faith cancel God's faithfulness? Not at all! Let God be true, and every man a liar." -Romans 3:3

Let God be true and every man a liar. Amen!

But to appease man's logic, ask yourself, who in their right mind would wait for something that they in their flesh don't want? If it wasn't for God, I would have moved on ten years ago. Who would wait over a decade for something that seems impossible? Who would keep believing when the evidence is stacked against them? Then there's the fact that I don't feel released to move on. Furthermore, I have not been attracted to any man in over ten years. God has kept me single and free of temptation for a reason.

What about the complete peace he gives me when I come in agreement with his promises? What about the conviction when I doubt? Really the only thing that's logical is the fact that this is God's plan, not mine. Sometimes it's actually faith that is the most logical. Faith often defies reason.

You have to understand that we don't fight flesh and blood. It's not people who come against you, it's demonic entities. And the enemy knows exactly how to target you in order to get the biggest reaction. We are in a spiritual battle fighting a very real devil who has a very real agenda.

> "For our fight is not against flesh and blood, but against the rulers, against the authorities, against the powers of this dark world and against the spiritual forces of evil in the heavenly realms." -Ephesians 6:12

There will always be the opinions of others but God has used every way possible to assure me that I am in his perfect will. It's his opinion that matters and he keeps me on track. I wake up with new supernatural grace every morning. Strength. Insight. Favor. Peace. Endurance. In every day and in every moment, God is so faithful to provide exactly what I need, just when I need it.

Not my will but yours be done, Lord.

God knows our end from our beginning and every detail in between. He knows every choice that we will make. He wouldn't have you hold on to his word just to fail you in the end. Keep fighting the good fight of faith my friend. If God said it, it will happen. Period.

> "No weapon formed against you shall prosper in Jesus name! He will condemn every tongue that has spoken against you." -Isaiah 54:17

With God on your side who can be against you? Nobody.

I know it's hard feeling isolated and misunderstood; rest assured, God is in your corner. Jesus was also isolated and misunderstood when he chose to obey his Father. We should not be surprised as believers when we face trials since we are called to follow in Christ's footsteps to "share in his sufferings and to carry our cross every day."

"Now if we are children, then we are heirs—heirs of God and co-heirs with Christ, if indeed we share in his sufferings in order that we may also share in his glory."
-Romans 8:17

Remember, it is all for His glory! Know that your obedience pleases the heart of God; he is well pleased and will give you the grace that you need to finish well.

God always works in mysterious and very intentional ways. He has a purpose for all that he allows and his promise is to redeem and restore. God will have the final say in your story my friend. You can be confident in this: God's promises are **YES & AMEN**.

"For no matter how many promises God has made, they are "Yes" in Christ. And so through him the "Amen" is spoken by us to the glory of God."
-2 Corinthians 1:20

"I remain confident of this: I will see the goodness of the LORD in the land of the living. Wait for the LORD; be strong and take heart and wait for the LORD."
-Psalms 27: 13-14

God's constant confirmation, discipline and supernatural grace gives me the endurance I need to run my race well. Yes, you read that right, his discipline. Why would I thank God for his discipline? We read in Hebrews, my favorite book of the Bible, for a better understanding.

"My child, don't make light of the Lord's discipline and do not lose heart when he rebukes you because the Lord disciplines those he loves. Endure hardship as discipline; God is treating you like his child. For what son is not disciplined by his father? Only his true son receives correction. God disciplines us for our good, that we may share in his holiness. No discipline is pleasant at the time but later it produces a harvest of righteousness and peace for those that are trained by it. So strengthen your body." -Hebrews 12

Every person on earth will suffer at some point in their life but not every person will have a positive outcome from that suffering. The devil has one purpose on this earth and that is to steal, kill and destroy. God's purpose is to restore and redeem. Enduring hardship has a purpose. God promises in Romans to work ALL things for good for those that love him. None of your pain is wasted. None of your suffering will lead to destruction. If you allow God to do the work that he needs to do in you, then you will share in his holiness, righteousness and peace. He uses discipline to perfect our faith.

"People who accept discipline are on the pathway to life, but those who ignore correction will go astray."
-Proverbs 10:17

God wants us to run this race with endurance, not limp all the way to the finish line. We were created to thrive, not merely survive.

"Let us throw off everything that hinders and the sin that so easily entangles and run with perseverance the race marked out for us, fixing our eyes on Jesus, the author and perfecter of our faith." -Hebrews 12: 1-2

Noah didn't stop building the ark to explain himself to every doubter and hater. Keep building and let the rain do the talking.

"Stop trusting in man who has but a breath in his nostrils. Of what account is he?" -Isaiah 2:22

People's opinions about you can change overnight. You must trust God over man. God never changes his mind about you.

Obedience to God may sometimes require you to disappoint the expectations of others.

I am enduring a spiritual labor season. There are people who instead of holding my hand as I carry, they want me to abort God's promises. But God has stepped in to bless me with purpose driven friends who have been like mid wives. They are in the room helping me push and give birth to my destiny and what a delivery it will be!

"You will grieve, but your grief will turn to joy. A woman giving birth to a child has pain because her time has come; but when her baby is born she forgets the anguish because of her joy that a child is born into the world. So with you: Now is your time of grief, but I will see you again and you will rejoice, and no one will take away your joy." -John 16:20-22

Stay laser focused so you won't be moved by the opposition. Fix your eyes on the only one that cannot lie, who never fails and is faithful to the end. God is literally out of this world good.

" Live to please an audience of *one*. "

SWEET TALKING IDOLS

If you are waiting for specific dreams and promises to come to pass then hold on, trust in God's perfect timing and plan. But don't hold on too tight.

Desires such as a mate, child, job, success, health and relationships are gifts from God and are not wrong in themselves, but when they take the place of God in our hearts then they have become an idol. We must be aware of any false gods each of us are allowing on the throne of our lives.

You may be thinking, I don't have idols and there is nothing I worship besides Jesus.

Ask yourself, what do you sacrifice for? What makes you mad? What do you worry about? What takes up your time?

Sweet talking idols might seem harmless but they are destructive. Our addictions such as social media, entertainment, food, money, achievement, romance, shopping and relationships can separate us from a right relationship with God.

"You shall not make for yourself an idol, or any likeness of what is in heaven above or on the earth below. For I, the Lord, your God, am a jealous God."
-Deut. 5:8-10

God wants you and not just some of you. He is jealous for your whole heart. It is important to recognize that idols can be good things that we have made ultimate things. An idol is anything that consumes us, controls us. Anything that takes the rightful place of God at the center of our lives. We can't expect things or people to fill a God-shaped void.

Idols are defeated not by being removed but by being replaced. In other words, Christ meets the need we seek to fill with idols.

Years ago, I had a revelation that even those God given desires and assignments can become idols. One night during dinner with a close friend, I started venting about my long season of waiting. Instead of sympathizing with me, she checked my attitude and she wasn't the only one.

The Holy Spirit also began to deal with me. I realized that the long years of waiting for God to fulfill the promises, the countless times I've shared my story, the ongoing opposition – it all took its toll on me.

When expectations are not met, it can lead to feelings of disappointment, frustration, and even anger. It became clear that what was once a source of joy and hope was now a heavy weight, a burden that I carried. I felt weary and hopeless. The call of God on my life became a false identity. I was holding tight to something that I never owned and God wanted it back. So I dropped to my knees,

"Lord, I repent for idolizing my promises."

After repenting, I felt God's good pleasure. I'm telling you friends, surrender is not a one-time deal.

He also gave a vision of me putting the promises on the alter, like Abraham did with Isaac. "God, none of this is mine. I release it. However and whenever you decide to do it is up to you. I surrender all. Satisfy my heart. Restore my joy."

When I gave the promises back to God and released my expectations, I saw breakthrough. Now I am walking out that breakthrough.

The difference between releasing our desires to the Lord and giving up is the posture of our hearts. The posture of our heart is trusting that he's going to work on our behalf while still praying and believing in his word. It's that surrender and trust that he requires and gives us freedom.

Sometimes it's a process so don't be hard on yourself. Ask Jesus for grace and to show you what you need to release. He will walk it out with you.

He is rooting for you and so am I.
Never stop praying!

"Be strong, and let your heart take courage, all you who wait for the Lord!" Isaiah 41:10 - "Fear not, for I am with you; be not dismayed, for I am your God; I will strengthen you, I will help you, I will uphold you with my righteous right hand." -Psalm 31:24

LENS OF FAITH

CHAPTER 8

FRUIT OF THE WILDNERNESS

As I finish writing my book and reflect on God's consistent goodness, my heart is filled with gratitude. God's faithfulness is proven on every page, every chapter and in every detail of my story. He did exactly what he said he would do in me all those years ago, "A new thing, you will never be the same." God himself has cultivated a thriving orchard in the middle of a desert. Here I share some of the life changing fruit from my journey of surrendering all.

I have covered all these topics more in depth and multiple times on my blog, podcast, Youtube channel and social media accounts, if you would like more.

1. FEAR OF THE LORD
2. QUICK CONVICTION
3. CAPTIVATING YOUR THOUGHTS
4. FREEDOM IN FORGIVENESS
5. SOUL TIES
6. DESIRING DISCERNMENT
7. CUTTING OUT THE MIDDLEMAN
8. MARY IN A MARTHA WORLD
9. DIVINE APPOINTMENTS
10. PURPOSE DRIVEN FRIENDS
11. PROTECTION NOT REJECTION
12. THE ONE
13. SINGLE AND SATISFIED
14. IDENTITY IN CHRIST

BONUS:

SPIRITUAL WARFARE PRAYER

FEAR OF THE LORD

I was raised in a Christian home and taught to fear the Lord. It kept me in line and out of major trouble but it was unhealthy.

I thought that God was watching my every move, ready to punish me. My idea of him was like a judge hitting his gavel down every time I disrespected my parents or did anything wrong. This brought on shame and kept me from intimacy with Jesus because I saw him as a stern father. I had the wrong view of who God truly is. It's his kindness that leads us to repentance.

"It is the riches of God's kindness and forbearance and patience, that leads you to repentance. -Romans 2:4

It's conviction, not condemnation. The Lord brings conviction. The devil brings condemnation and shame. We are meant to have the fear of the Lord that is motivated by love and reverence, not fear of punishment. We should want to please Jesus because we love him.

The word of God brings life and understanding!

"The Lord delights in those who fear him, who put their hope in his unfailing love." -Psalm 147:11

"The fear of the Lord is the beginning of wisdom; all who follow his precepts have good understanding. To him belongs eternal praise." -Psalm 111:10

"In the fear of the Lord there is strong confidence, and his children will have a place of refuge." -Proverbs 14:26

"Humility is the fear of the Lord; its wages are riches and honor and life." -Proverbs 22:4

"Blessed are all who fear the Lord, who walk in obedience to him." -Psalm 128:1

"The fear of the Lord leads to life; then one rests content, untouched by trouble." -Proverbs 19:23

QUICK CONVICTION

Our hearts are easily deceived and pride will have us convinced that we are "good enough." Our goal as believers should not be to live in the "gray" area but instead to live pleasing the Lord. That means we don't want to entertain things that pollute our spirits and give the devil access.

These things include worldly movies, music, negative words and thoughts, wrong relationships, idols, compromise and unforgiveness.

You can't slay demons when you're entertaining them.

Ask the Holy Spirit to give you his quick conviction. Like the fear of the Lord, quick conviction keeps us protected and right with God. Begin to starve the flesh in order to feed the spirit, because you can't be flesh fed and spirit led. When your spirit is full and satisfied, you will no longer crave junk. What was once a temptation, becomes unpleasant and then offensive. You want nothing to do with the things that pollute your spirit.

In order to live in this freedom, you must stay guarded by keeping the armor of God on every day.

"Put on the full armor of God, so that you can take your stand against the devil's schemes. For our struggle is not against flesh and blood, but against the rulers, against the authorities, against the powers of this dark world and against the spiritual forces of evil in the heavenly realms. Therefore, put on the full armor of God, so that when the day of evil comes, you may be able to stand your ground. Stand firm then, with the belt of truth buckled around your waist, with the breastplate of righteousness in place, and with your feet with the fitted with the readiness that comes from the gospel of peace. In addition to all this, take up the shield of faith, with which you can extinguish all the flaming arrows of the evil one. Take the helmet of salvation and the sword of the Spirit, which is the Word of God. And pray in the Spirit on all occasions with all kinds of prayers and requests." -Ephesians 6: 10-18

There is a relationship between believers and the Holy Spirit that is precious. Something we don't think about a lot is that the Holy Spirit is deeply in love with us. He wants to reveal Himself to us, but when we act independently from God's principles, we grieve the Holy Spirit.

If we deliberately do something wrong, we drag Him into the mire of sin with us. We need to be aware that the Holy Spirit lives in us and honor Him by confessing our sin and receive cleansing by the blood of Jesus so our fellowship will be restored with the Spirit of God.

Like I mentioned before, there is a difference in conviction and condemnation. Conviction is a gift from the Lord. Condemnation is a tool of the enemy's that is meant to cause shame. The Lord loves you and wants to keep you on the right path of righteousness. But he is never out to get you or make you feel worthless. He lovingly convicts us to warn us. His conviction leads us to repentance which keeps our hearts free of anything that could separate us from him and cause us harm.

We serve a good, good father that wants us to live our best life!

CAPTIVATING YOUR THOUGHTS

Do you know how powerful your thought life is? Every positive or negative act starts with a single thought. Mental torment is from the devil and is the main tool that he uses to try and defeat us. If the enemy can control your mind, then he can control your life.

When my marriage fell apart, the enemy would constantly remind me of the rejection and pain that I experienced. Sometimes, I would go throughout the entire day replaying painful memories which would trigger anger and resentment. The devil had a hay day on my mind, leaving me with no peace. The good news is that God always gives us a way out.

One day very clearly, the Holy Spirit told me to "Fight back. Captivate your thoughts." Then he pointed me to what is now one of my life verses. I memorized it and now declare this powerful statement over my mind every day:

"We demolish arguments and every pretension that sets itself up against the knowledge of God, and we take captive every thought to make it obedient to Christ."
-2 Corinthians 10:5

It is good to be proactive and declare this verse first thing every day. Of course, this tool isn't a magic wand. If you are filling your mind with garbage, living in sin or carrying offense in your heart then you need to get that right first. But if you are otherwise being targeted with constant negative thoughts, lies or time-wasting distractions then trade that in for peace.

Even positive thoughts can keep us distracted from spending time with God or completing the assignment he has called us to. Once we understand how powerful our thoughts and words are then we can be aware and take the necessary steps to captivate them.

We have a real enemy and it's not people. We are fighting the powers of darkness, the tormenting demons who use people as vessels just like God uses people as vessels for his kingdom. We are in a spiritual battle of good vs. evil. In order to win the mental battle, we must know how to target and disarm the enemy.

"Put on the full armor of God, so that you can take your stand against the devil's schemes. For our struggle is not against flesh and blood, but against the rulers, against the authorities, against the powers of this dark world and against the spiritual forces of evil in the heavenly realms." -Ephesians 6:11

If you don't fill your mind with God's word, the enemy will fill it with stress, anxiety, negativity and temptation.

Once I started captivating my thoughts, I experienced supernatural peace and freedom.

Whereas before, my mind roamed with toxic thoughts which led to restless night's sleep and then I'd wake up in a bad mood. All because of past offenses that I wanted to forget. Now anytime the enemy tries to mess with my mind, I immediately put my hands on my head and declare, "Lord, captivate my thoughts."

Watch God intervene, as you open your mouth and fight back. Declaring the verse 2 Corinthians 10:5 is like hitting the emergency brake during a high-speed chase. Instead of giving the enemy your time and energy, you can stop him immediately. As you continue to walk in your God-given authority, you defeat the enemy and he moves on. Because he only preys on the weak but you are strong in Christ.

You decide what thoughts get to pitch a tent and make camp in your head. You are the mayor of your mind. Time to evict the lies and welcome the truth.

You've got power over the enemy because Jesus Christ, the all-powerful One lives in you. You have no need to worry or fear!

"Do not conform to the pattern of this world, but be transformed by the renewing of your mind. Then you will be able to test and approve what God's will is—his good, pleasing and perfect will." -Romans 12:2

5 Practical Steps to Transform Your Mind and Replace Negative Thoughts

1. Train your brain to recognize false beliefs or negative thoughts.
2. Call out the negative thoughts or lies. (2 Corinthians 10:5)
3. Replace lies with truth.
4. Study and meditate on Scripture.
5. Pray.

FREEDOM IN FORGIVENESS

There's a well-known saying that goes, "Unforgiveness is like drinking deadly poison, expecting the other person to die."

When we are not quick to release offense, it affects us most of all. Your offender has power over you until you let them go. Harboring offense not only effects all of our relationships but most importantly it separates us from a right relationship with God. God says that when you don't truly forgive from the depth of your heart then he himself will not forgive you.

"If you forgive other people when they sin against you, your heavenly Father will also forgive you. But if you do not forgive others their sins, your Father God will not forgive your sins." -Matthew 6:14

This alone should motivate us to release offenses. There's a reason that God instructs us to be quick to forgive. The longer you wait to forgive, the harder it is for you to forgive.

"Be even-tempered, content with second place, quick to forgive an offense. Forgive as quickly and completely as the Master forgave you." -Colossians 3:12

Unforgiveness if not resolved leads to bitterness, which impacts you relationally, mentally, emotionally, spiritually and yes even physically. Many physical problems have their roots in spiritual issues, primarily in the area of unforgiveness. I help lead a healing ministry, where a team of us pray for the sick. It's amazing how often the simple act of forgiving someone from their past is the key to their physical healing. I've seen God instantly heal bodies and hearts as soon as someone chooses to repent and forgive.

To take it a step further, God commands us to bless those that hurt us.

"To you who are listening I say: Love your enemies, do good to those who hate you, bless those who curse you, pray for those who mistreat you." -Matthew 5:44

This is next level but it's so freeing. It keeps your heart unclogged, it stops the devil from gaining access into your life and it gives you peace. Choose to forgive and bless those that offend you.

SOUL TIES

You can have healthy and unhealthy soul ties. For example, the close friendship of David and Jonathan. They had a close brotherly friendship. There are positive and negative bonds that we create but we should never allow them to control us. We must recognize the difference by allowing the Holy Spirit to reveal what is godly and what is not.

A common misconception is that soul ties are just sexual. Even though strong bonds are created from intimacy, they are not the only way a tie is formed.

Powerful ties can be linked to parents, business partners, friendships, siblings, leaders, pastors and even things.

It is the joining or knitting together of two with the same purpose or heart. You can have a good soul tie such as in, marriage or godly friends. There are also negative or ungodly ties, that will bring you into bondage, rob you of your will or is harmful.

> "For freedom Christ has set us free; stand firm therefore, and do not submit again to a yoke of slavery."-Galatians 5:1

DESIRING DISCERNMENT

This is one of the most important lessons that God has taught me and walking in it has changed me. I did not always desire discernment because I wanted to live ignorant, head in the clouds and just focus on being happy, which is a form of escapism. But part of maturing in Christ is the desire to know what is really going on. When you know better, you do better.

It's easy to see that we are living in crazy times. We are in a culture that calls good evil and evil good. We are watching the devil run these streets, bolder and louder than ever while the church has been silent. But God is calling us to wake up and speak up. To take a stand for righteousness.

You can't defeat a 24/7 devil by being a part time Christian.

To be sensitive to the Lord's leading requires discernment and wisdom. Discernment also keeps us out of harms way. Being able to discern who, what and how is crucial, and it keeps us protected. Ask God to give you discernment, wisdom and be sensitive to his prompting.

You can't be sneaky around people that have discernment. We are either going to dream it, feel it, smell it, hear it or see it. God will reveal one way or another.

"Who is wise? Let them realize these things. Who is discerning? Let them understand." -Hosea 14:9

"Preserve sound judgement and discernment, do not let them out of your sight. They will be life for you, an ornament around your neck. Then you will be safe and will not fall. Have no fear of sudden disaster or of the ruin that overtakes the wicked, for the Lord will be at your side and will keep your foot from being snared."

-Proverbs 3

CUTTING OUT THE MIDDLEMAN

I remember one day while I was shopping at my favorite grocery store, Trader Joe's, while admiring their creative wall art a quote jumped out at me. "We can offer you high quality at low prices because we cut out the middleman."

I was so curious to know more so I asked a cashier what that meant. She told me that most markets hire a buyer who then goes to the farmer but Trader Joe's instead goes straight to the farmers. This saves on costs which gives them the ability to offer us high quality groceries at low prices.

I thought, what a great idea. Then one day as I was watching sermons on Youtube, the Lord reminded me of that day in the store and said, "Cut out the middleman."

You see, there are many amazing men and women of God who minister to us. But no matter how anointed your favorite musician, pastor, prophet, youtuber or author is, they are merely a messenger for the kingdom.

Don't become more familiar with God's people than with God himself.

I love powerful spirit led music that ushers us into God's presence but we don't need the perfect worship song to connect with him. I have often discovered greater intimacy in the times that I sing out a new love song from my heart or press in without help from a middleman. Nurture a deeper relationship with Jesus that doesn't require another humans anointing.

Think of this analogy, say you are sitting across from someone you love and you're reading them this beautifully worded Hallmark card that you picked out and bought just for them. They would probably smile and say thank you. But what if instead, you are sitting across from that person you love, staring deep into their eyes and then begin gushing just how much you adore them. You're not repeating something that someone else already said. Instead, it's your own authentic and original words that are flowing from your heart. That would actually deepen your relationship. You see, the Hallmark card, no matter how wonderful, is still the middleman.

There are times to turn off the noise, remove the distractions, sit before our King and pour *our own* oil at his feet.

MARY IN A MARTHA WORLD

We must make spending time with Jesus our priority because life is full of distractions. We can exhaust ourselves with our never-ending to-do lists. But Jesus teaches us a valuable lesson with the story of Lazarus's sisters, Mary and Martha.

Martha was a doer, very task oriented, so when she heard that Jesus and his crew were coming to visit, she got on the move. She frantically got her house in order, cooking, cleaning, striving for perfection. I know us women can relate, right.

On the other hand, her sister Mary wasn't helping at all. She just wanted to be with Jesus, to sit as His feet and hear what he had to say. Martha in her frustration, goes and complains to Jesus, hoping he will help her out and put Mary in check.

Instead, Jesus responds,

"Martha, you are worried and upset by many things, yet only one thing is needed, Mary has chosen what is better and it will not be taken away from her." But what about the meal, the tasks, the calendar, the schedule?

Only one thing is needed.

Even though we all have daily responsibilities and tasks that are important, we can often make working more of a priority than just being. If we are honest with ourselves, we spend far too much time being entertained by tv, social media and doing activities that can wait.

Jesus is calling us to *do the better thing.*

DIVINE APPOINTMENTS

Far too many Christians have the belief that once they say the sinner's prayer, they receive their "golden ticket" to heaven and then nothing else is required. But we were created for a purpose and it's not to live a self-centered life. Jesus chose to endure such torment and be nailed to a cross, not just to save mankind but that we would become his kingdom change agents. Jesus surrendered all so that we would surrender all. Our mission on this earth should be his mission which is to **build his eternal kingdom over our temporary kingdom.**

When we are so focused on our plans and our clock we miss out on those greater opportunities. The funny thing is that out of all the times that God has interrupted my schedule for a divine appointment, it has never prevented me from doing what I need. It's like God adds time to the clock.

"Your heavenly Father knows what you need. But seek first the kingdom of God and his righteousness, and all these things will also be given to you."

-Matthew 6:32-33

Once I surrendered all, God began to give me his heart for people. Now I pray for divine appointments every morning, and every day he brings them my way. Now life is one big Jesus adventure and I love it.

I've had divine appointments while shopping at the grocery store, at the gym, on a phone call, even by commenting on a social media post. I've led people to salvation from just one dm on social media. God can and will use anything for his kingdom's sake (remember the mascara?)

Life surrendered to Jesus is never boring! There is so much joy and feeling of purpose that comes from a God setup.

We are alive on this earth for a short while; we really are not promised tomorrow, so let's get over ourselves and make the most of every opportunity.

"Be very careful, then, how you live-not as unwise but as wise, making the most of every opportunity, because the days are evil. Therefore do not be foolish, but understand what the Lord's will is."
-Ephesians 5: 15-17

I'm reminded of the time I went with my friend to a grocery store just to quickly pick up her birthday balloons. The man running the counter was an emotional wreck. He was slipping on water, popping balloons and acting very anxious. Then he looks over at us and says, "I'm having the worst day ever."

In that moment, I felt to ask if I could pray for him. So we joined together right there to pray and encourage him, and even invited him to church. He said that we made his day so much better as he stayed smiling ear to ear. This is an example of a divine appointment.

They can happen anywhere and anytime, but we must be flexible and ready to go when the opportunity presents itself.

We live in a lost and broken world that needs a Savior. God has called us to be his hands and feet.

"How will people call on Jesus in whom they have not believed? And how will they believe in him of whom they have not heard? And how will they hear without a messenger? Just as it is written and forever remains written, **"How beautiful are the hands and feet of those who bring the good news!"** -Romans 10:15

PURPOSE DRIVEN FRIENDS

As a funny and outgoing extrovert, it has always been easy for me to make friends and with a variety of different crowds. Regularly hanging out and having fun was what I loved to do.

But fast forward to God telling me, "I'm going to do a new thing, not a revised version but a NEW thing in you." The first thing he had to do was uproot the need to be liked.

Relationships were a false identity and an idol in my life. I even remember telling God one day, "You can have it all Lord, just don't take my people." So now you know exactly what he needed to deal with first.

When I gave God permission to do the real work in my life, he began removing everything that was comfortable and familiar to me, like popularity. He began to remove those relationships that would no longer be beneficial to where he was taking me.

You see, when God is taking you higher, to a place you've never been, not everybody can come with you. Not everyone is built for the journey. In addition, many people can only relate to your broken, immature self. They will no longer be attracted to you as you heal and mature in Christ. Remember, unhealthy attracts unhealthy. Staying attached to the wrong people can actually hinder you from moving forward. I have learned that most friends are seasonal, few are lifetime. Allow God to decide who's best for you and how long they stay.

God was about to shake things up in my life big time. He intentionally moved me across the country, to live in an unfamiliar and uncomfortable place. He kept me isolated for years. I felt invisible. When he first moved me, my friends and family would say, "Leah, you'll make friends really quick. You always do. You never met a stranger. You'll have fun." But God was like, nope. Not this time. I'm doing a new thing.

For example, I would go to an event and meet someone; we'd hit it off and plan to get coffee but then she would totally ghost me. No call, no text, nothing. Or I would meet with a potential friend one time but then never hear from them again. It was so strange. I would try and make sense of why I couldn't make friends. It's probably this culture. My personality doesn't fit in here.

Maybe it's because of my story. Maybe it's because my marriage fell apart. Then God made it clear that he was the one preventing those friendships. He said, "I didn't move you here to collect friends and become distracted with fun. Let me choose your relationships and who you spend time with."

Remember, God's ways are not our ways. We naturally choose friends based on commonalities. As if to say, we have these five things in common, oh we should be friends. And if we're honest, we selfishly only want to spend time with people that make us feel good or who meet our needs. But those types of relationships are often shallow and conditional. A God connection has a very different and deeper purpose.

"As iron sharpens iron, so one friend sharpens another." -Proverbs 27:17

When God began choosing my friends, he would connect me with women that I would never naturally click with. We didn't have similar personalities, backgrounds, interests or life stages. But God isn't concerned with that, he joins us to specific people for our good and his glory. He has an eternal agenda. Remember, God's ways are much different than ours.

Not saying that you won't enjoy who God brings into your life, it's just that fun is not his priority. His intention for relationships is to serve, encourage, be accountable and to challenge you to be more like Jesus and fulfill his greater purposes.

DAVID AND JONATHAN

One of my most valued purpose driven friends is Rae. As a wife, a busy mother of four young children and a total introvert, we don't naturally relate to each other. Rae and I actually have very little in common, in fact, we don't even like the same pizza. But we have one thing in common. It's really the most important thing that matters in any relationship and that is we both love and serve Jesus whole heartedly.

I can't express enough how much Rae has been a total God send! She has been a faithful rock, a hard truth teller, my ride or die, my personal prayer warrior and when I needed one the most. I tell her that if it wasn't for her, I might have given up during that time of heartache and isolation. I credit my inner healing and even thriving today, partly due to our friendship.

God knows exactly what you need to complete your assignment. It's important to surround yourself with the right people. Surround yourself with people who pray for you behind your back. God will bring you saints that believe with you, encourage you to keep going no matter how impossible it seems, to pray without ceasing, stick closest and aren't swayed by the opinions of others. I thank God for these ones.

But then there's a Jonathan type of friendship.

Jonathan was David's best friend. The Bible says, "the soul of Jonathan was knit to the soul of David, and Jonathan loved Him as His own soul."

Rae is my Jonathan. Even as a very busy mom with four young children, all under the age of five, God would stop her mid task to encourage me. There were times that she would wake up in the middle of the night with prophetic visions or she would stop in the middle of her busy schedule to cry out for me.

Rae had one free hour a day, while her kiddos were napping and that's when I would come over, once a week. It was my divine appointment. There were times, I would come over feeling depressed while venting that this is too hard and I want to give up. Then we would pray together and God would often give her a word of encouragement for me. Rae would constantly remind me of God's promises when I felt overwhelmed and we would both engage in spiritual warfare. Any tormenting spirit would flee when we were together. By the time I left her house, I was always refreshed and ready to keep going.

Another thing, a David and Jonathan type of friendship is unbreakable because this bond is not about you. Those shallow and conditional relationships often don't stand the test of time. If there is offense, they might walk out of your life. But a Jonathan friend is steadfast, understanding that they are tied to your destiny. Thank God for purpose driven friendships!

PROTECTION NOT REJECTION

I covered some of this earlier in Chapter 2.

We have all felt the sting of rejection at some point, usually starting from childhood. Whether it stems from abandonment, slander, being uninvited, excluded or abused. The spirit of rejection can go deep.

During the time that God was teaching me the value of purpose driven friends, he also gave me another powerful revelation. Here I was still healing from abandonment by my husband. Then God moved me across the country, where I was separated from all my family and friends. Then on top of that, I wasn't making any new friends. During that season of isolation, there were times that I might have even felt rejected by God.

One day, I was feeling rejected because once again a potential friend ghosted me. It was then that the Holy Spirit reminded me of his protection.

There's nothing like having God's perspective. He began to show me that the reason certain people are not attached to me is because they would cause me more harm than good. If God wanted them to be in my life, then they would be. If he wanted you to be invited to the event, then you'd be there. If he wanted you to have what you're praying for, then you would have it.

When God gives you access, no man can shut the door. Nothing can stop what God has for you. The same is for when God denies access, no man can give it. Trust him with the open and shut doors. God is for you, not against you.

"The key of the house of David I will lay on his shoulder. Then he shall open, and no one shall shut. And he shall shut, and no one shall open." -Isaiah 22:22

The enemy tries to immediately harass us with a spirit of rejection when all the while it's God's great love and protection on our lives. Instead of allowing resentment to take root, thank God for keeping you out of harm's way.

How to Battle the Spirit of Rejection

John 10:10 tells us that these oppressive spirits from the enemy come to steal, kill, and destroy. They do this by persecuting you through your thoughts and bringing on fears and negative mindsets full of anxiety and depression.

- **Begin by prayerfully asking the Holy Spirit to reveal the root cause of this oppressive spirit.** He will often take you back to a memory, a moment when you made an agreement. God transforms us by renewing our minds, and that includes healing our memories. He sometimes heals slowly and will move gently. Be open to how He wants to reveal the root of rejection in your life, trusting Him to restore what's been stolen from you.

- **Repent of the areas and times you have believed the spirit of rejection and the orphan spirit over the spirit of sonship.** Take each thought the Holy Spirit reveals to you captive. Renounce it. God has sent the Spirit of His Son into your heart, the Spirit Who cries out, "Abba, Father" (Galatians 4:6). Ask the Spirit of Jesus within you to call on your Heavenly Father for rescue–He will help you begin to believe and know that you belong to Him.

- **Declare your identity in Jesus.** He has made you a new creation in Him. The old is gone, the new has come. The places of shame and regret the enemy has tried to tie you to no longer have a hold on you. Declare the power of the new thing God is doing in your life!

- **Stay in the Word of God.** Remember, in consistency lies the victory! Spend time with God daily and meditate, filling your mind with who He says you are. Journal scriptures the Holy Spirit highlights to you. Consider writing them on notecards and putting them in places you'll see regularly – specifically ones that speak of your new identity in Jesus as a son or daughter of God, forever accepted by Him!

- **Thank God for all He has done and will do as He promises to set you free.** As a Believer in Jesus, the Spirit of God is within you. And where He is, there is freedom! (2 Corinthians 3:17) As you surrender more to Him each day, you'll experience the fulfillment of this promise.

THE ONE

This God encounter literally shook me to my core.

It was during the time when he had me move from my own apartment to renting a room. Up until that point, I'd never had a roommate before, I've always had my own place. At first, this did not make much sense, it seemed like taking a step backward.

I looked everywhere for a room to rent in my part of town but there was nothing available at that time. Then a place opens up, but it's a renovated garage with 2 rooms, no windows, a makeshift kitchen and in a sketchy part of town. Shortly after moving in, I find out that the landlord is so disrespectful, that he turns over tenants every couple of months.

Within a few months a new roommate moves in, she's a woman in her twenties with a large dog. It's immediately evident that she's a lost soul, emotionally unstable and thrives on drama. She drank every day, brought home men for one-night stands, fought with the landlord and the list goes on. Every night after work, she would storm in like a tornado and start venting about her day as I sat there listening. I tried to offer her support and share the hope of Jesus, I even brought her to church one Sunday, but after months of chaos, I was drained and fed up. It felt like God was giving me the short end of the stick.

One afternoon, in my frustration I started pacing the room and questioning God,
"Why did you move me here?!? To this side of town, this landlord, in this garage, with this girl! Why am I here??"

His response marked me.

"I brought you here for her. Don't you ever forget how much I love THE ONE. I would move heaven and earth for THE ONE. I would die for THE ONE."

The power of his words hit me and I lost it as I sat down speechless, weeping, my room full of Jesus sweet presence.

He stamped that powerful life changing truth onto the bottom of my heart and now I don't see people the same.

As a Christian we know that Jesus loves people and he died for us, but when he actually shows you how great his love is, you're forever marked.

"I would leave the 99 to go rescue **the one** lost."

-Matthew 18:12-13

Oh, how Jesus loves you.

Our Savior has a different measuring stick then we do. In a world that places more value on quantity, Jesus says, "Hey I would stop everything for the one and so should you."

Jesus loves that one totally lost, sinful soul so much that he literally rearranged my life just for her. Let that sink in.

We often get caught up in thinking that numbers define success, but God's not impressed. He's not concerned with how much money you make, how many followers you have or by how many people attend your church. In fact, I've seen that the more something grows, the harder it becomes to see the one. And then you become the one you're focused on. But Jesus will always leave the masses to chase after the one in need.

He wants us to have his heart for the broken, lost and hurting. They are desperate for real love, real hope and we have the answer.

At the time, I did not understand why God put me in that living situation. I thought God was holding back his blessings. But one day after sharing my situation with a fellow minister, she says, "God must really trust you to place you there. Not everybody would have handled it the way you did."

So, instead of holding back his blessings, he was actually using me to be a blessing. Having God's perspective in every situation really does change everything.

God doesn't ever want us to lose sight of how much he values every single one of his creations.

Oh and I find it interesting that in one of the worst conditions, God birthed my ministry. It was in the fall of 2016, as I was sitting at my computer in that garage when God tells me to start blogging and says, "This will be the beginning of your ministry."

He named it, Lens of Faith.

So often the most important key moments in our lives occur during the hardest seasons. Jesus gives us beauty for ashes.

> "Don't ever forget how much I love *the one*. I would move heaven and earth for *the one*. I would die for *the one*."

SINGLE AND SATISFIED

We live in a society that tells singles that we are missing out but the truth is we are missing him. Even well-meaning folks in the church can make a single person feel like they are not complete or cannot be truly used by God until they are married with a family. It's just not true. You are not less-than. God has a purpose for keeping you to himself until you're ready. He's in the waiting and he wants your undivided attention, your heart, affection and your time.

A romantic relationship, no matter how great will never satisfy your deepest longing. And that is by God's intentional design. He created you with a void that only he can fill. So often singles deepest desire is for an imperfect person to knock us off our feet and romance us. When all the while the only perfect lover, your true soulmate, Jesus is sitting by your side 24/7. He is wooing you and waiting patiently for you to choose him.

Jesus isn't your temporary fill in until something better comes along. He is the definition of fulfillment. He is the best lover and friend you could have. If you are not content being single, then you may have made the desire to be married/have a family an idol in your life. The posture of your heart should be to give that desire back to God while you continue to pray with expectation.

Every season is a blessing whether you're single, married, with children or grandchildren. But the beauty of being single is the ability to focus on your relationship with Jesus without constant distractions.

I hear from my friends who have young families of their own, "I want to read my Bible but I'm always being pulled. I don't have alone time like when I was single."

Now of course, they love being married with children but when it's just you, there's simply more freedom and flexibility. You have the ability to just pick up and go without the responsibilities that come with having a family. You have the opportunity to strengthen a deeper love relationship with Jesus, to be fully dependent on him and to complete the tasks that he has called you too. The grass isn't greener on the other side. There are challenges that come with every season that God has us in.

Trust that God is preparing you during this time. He may still have work to do in your heart, to mature your character, he may have an assignment you need to complete solo first, he may be preparing your mate.

Don't run ahead of him. Settling for good enough out of impatience and loneliness may result in heartbreak. **Women don't need a knight in shining armor. They need a man covered in the full armor of God.**

Let the Lord fill any void so that you desire a mate that resembles your first love. The one who loved you first, and the only perfect lover is Jesus Christ. There are no substitutes that satisfy.

Ask the Lord what he wants to do in and through you in this single season to position you for the right partner in his perfect timing.

Know that Jesus loves you deeply and cares about the desires of your heart. Trust him. Everything really will come together and prove to be beautiful. When God writes your love story, it's worth the wait.

IDENTITY IN CHRIST

Insecurity comes when we find our identity in anything but Christ.

Everything changes once we really believe in who we are in Christ. Having your identity tied to status, your job title, ministry role, or who others say you are is shaky ground. It breeds insecurity, comparison and striving.

People pleasing and fear of man will keep you stuck. It causes you to be an emotional yo-yo powered by self-doubt. But when you truly walk in your God given identity, steady confidence follows. The opinions of man, the losses and gains of this world will not determine how you see yourself. Because your confidence will not come from self or a temporary outside source. Instead it comes from who you are in Christ. When you see yourself how he sees you, your foundation is no longer shaky.

We must keep a heart posture of humility, knowing that apart from Jesus Christ we are nothing. But because we are sons and daughters of King Jesus, we are royalty.

Anything good in us is because of who he is in us so God gets all the glory all of the time.

"We put no confidence in ourselves. Let the one who boasts, boast in the Lord. For it is not the one who honors himself who is approved, but the one whom the Lord honors." -2 Corinthians 10

You can walk in firm confidence, knowing that you are more than a conqueror in Jesus Christ!

These important life lessons have made me who I am today. You can learn more on each of these topics found in the Lens of Faith ministries blog, podcast and Youtube archives. Visit Leahmariecarson.com

"Insecurity comes when we find our identity in *anything* but Christ."

CHAPTER 9

DON'T GIVE UP

I would not be able to endure, mature and thrive in this long valley if it weren't for God's supernatural grace on my life. His grace takes what would otherwise be impossible and makes it all possible.

God has a bigger plan for your life than you do on your own.

I encourage you to say yes and partner with him. Follow his leading and obey him every step of the way. When God says go, trust and obey. When it seems too hard, lean on his faithfulness.

He is the only one with perfect character. His track record is flawless. If I had even 1% of doubt in who God is, I would have given up many years ago.

When it seems like nobody is cheering you on, you must keep your eyes laser focused on the one who never doubts and is faithful to the end. He is cheering you on. Jesus Christ the King and the Creator of the universe is cheering you on and he is your defender.

I'm sure you can imagine that with a faith journey like mine, I have faced the enemy's fierce attempts on my life. I have taken the hits. It's true, he wants nothing more than for me to lose hope and give up on my destiny. Because he knows the impact I will make on my generation, for the kingdom of God. So I must keep my armor on and fight back.

The devil will never admit it, but the reason he wants you to give up is because he believes every word God has spoken about you.

The devil won't win unless you let him. You must show him how defeated he really is. Instead of believing the lies of the enemy, declare God's truth.

I always say, the devil is just a mouse with a microphone. He's really loud but he has no power.

The only power he has is the power you give him. You must walk in your God given authority, knowing that you are more than a conquer in Christ. If God is for you, who can be against you? NOBODY.

The Lord is faithful so you can stay faithful. He has never failed you and he won't start now. He keeps his promises. His ways are not your ways and thank God for that. His ways are better. His timing is perfect. God's dreams for you are so much bigger than you could imagine. This is Bible truth.

If you are waiting for God to come through on promises that you know without a doubt are from him then hold on my friend. If you feel discouraged and weary, I understand, I've been there. But don't lose hope. There is a purpose for the wait and no time is wasted when you are following his lead.

Don't allow your heart to harden in your long season. Get on your knees, even now, and give it all to the one that holds every tear, every dream and every minute with his tender loving care.

"The devil is just a *mouse* with a *microphone.*"

CHAPTER 10

LIVE YOUR BEST LIFE

Just like those in the hall of faith, God has a great destiny and purpose planned for your life. But first he is waiting on you to surrender all and partner with him.

Give him permission to go deep, to uproot and heal you of any emotional soul wounds so there is nothing holding you back. A couple of the issues that will keep you stuck is fear of man and people pleasing. That really has to go.

I know it is not easy but you must put in the work in order to have the reward of lasting fruit. Healthy fruit will not grow without water, soil, sun, nutrients and care.

Allow God to refine you so that you will reflect his image and his heart. God wants to mold and shape you into his likeness. The process will start out uncomfortable, like pruning is expected to be. But if you don't give up there is sure to blossom a beautiful life-giving tree with much healthy fruit. That fruit will change lives and impact generations to come. It's worth it. Your life will never be the same. You really were born for such a time as this and your best is yet to come.

I pray that my story encourages you and increases your faith. I pray that you will surrender all so that you can live your best life.

I am praying for you and cheering you on!
with love, Leah

I'm including a powerful spiritual warfare prayer as you turn the next page. This prayer has blessed many and I get messages telling me how these declarations have changed people's circumstances. Praise God!

LENS OF FAITH

SPIRITUAL WARFARE PRAYER

Prayer for breakthrough:

As your servant, Oh God, I confess my continued allegiance and surrender myself completely in every area of my life. I cover myself and my family with the blood of Jesus for our protection. And I take a stand against all the workings of Satan and his demons that would hinder me or any family member.

I place upon myself, with thanksgiving, the Armor You have provided: The Girdle of Truth, The Breastplate of Righteousness, The Sandals of Peace, The Shield of Faith, and the Helmet of Salvation. And I take up the Sword of The Spirit.

By faith and dependence upon You I put off all fleshy works of the old man and stand in the victory of the cross where Jesus provided cleansing from the old man and has provided a way for me to live above sin.

Heavenly Father, I give You thanks that I am seated in the heavenlies, and I recognize by faith that all wicked (demonic) spirits and Satan himself are under my feet and are subject to me in the name of Jesus.

Father, I thank You that the weapons of our warfare are not carnal but mighty through God for pulling down strongholds. To casting down imaginations and every high thing that exalts itself against the knowledge of God, and to bring every thought into obedience to the Lord Jesus Christ.

Therefore, in my life today, I will tear down the strongholds of Satan and smash his plans that have been formed against me. Tearing down the strongholds of Satan against my mind, and I surrender my mind to the Holy Spirit. I affirm that my heavenly Father did not give me a spirit of fear, but a spirit of power, of love and a sound mind. So I break and smash the strongholds of Satan formed against my emotions today. I give my emotions to You.

I smash the strongholds of Satan formed against my will today. Lord, I give my will to You, and choose to make the right decisions of faith and obedience. Therefore, I smash the strongholds of Satan formed against my body, and I declare that no diseases, no germ, bacteria, virus or illness of any kind can live on or in this body. I give my body to You Father recognizing that I am Your temple and I rejoice in Your mercy and goodness.

I Decree and Declare:
All works of the enemy that are contrary to or would hinder the fulfillment of God's plan and purpose in my life are broken. I am liberated from all generational, spoken or satanic curses. I sever them by the sword (Word of God), the Spirit and the blood.

I am free from any and all demonic influences that negatively affect me physically, emotionally, psychologically, spiritually or by any other means. The wisdom of God directs my life and cannot be twisted or perverted in any way.

Neither Satan nor his fallen angels have any right to my finances and all the wealth of the wicked comes to me now. I command Satan to cough it up, spit it out and let it go. Satan cannot cause confusion nor interfere with my hearing the voice of God regarding my daily ministry assignment.

I will stand in victory against all attacks of the enemy and will destroy all attempts to deceive me, to ambush me or to interfere with my assigned ministry.

Through prayer, worship and obedience to God I will continue to defeat Satan and his unclean spirits.

In the name of Jesus, I repent of, bind up, rebuke, cast out, nullify, and forbid off myself, my wife/husband, my family, my friends, my church, and my community the following demonic spirits.

Spirit of poverty; religious & pharisaical spirits; mindsets of lack, worry & fear; spirits of witchcraft & control; selfishness; spirits of lust & sexual immorality; pride; fear & timidity; self-righteousness; spirits of apathy & luke warmness; negative thoughts and ideas; rebellion; depression; compromise with the world; intimidation; discouragement; accusation; self-gratification; spirits of death & suicide; and all spirits associated with mental, emotional or physical illness.

I pull down every generational curse, all hexes and word curses and call all my relationships into Godly order. I decree and declare my life is under and in the order of God Almighty.

Father, I pray that now and through this day You would strengthen and enlighten me. Show me the ways Satan is hindering and tempting and lying and distorting the truth in my life. Enable me to be aggressive mentally, to think about and practice Your Word. And give You, Your rightful place in my life.

I pray that the Holy Spirit would bring all the work of the crucifixion. All the work of the resurrection, all the work of the glorification, and all the work of Pentecost into my life today.

In Jesus' name this life You have given me, is Yours completely. My God is Jehovah and He is the God who saves, heals and delivers. Therefore, I refuse to be discouraged, to worry or to speak negatively. You are the God of hope. Teach me to speak blessings and not curses. You have proven Your power by resurrecting Jesus from the dead. So, I claim in every way this power and victory over all satanic forces in my life.

I pray this prayer in the name of the Lord Jesus Christ with thanksgiving. I seal this prayer by the blood of the lamb. In Jesus name Amen.

LENS OF FAITH
ministries
—— LEAH MARIE CARSON ——

LENS OF FAITH® MINISTRIES OFFERS MANY FREE RESOURCES THAT ARE AVAILABLE TO EQUIP YOU ON YOUR FAITH JOURNEY. SUBSCRIBE AND FOLLOW FOR POWERFUL TESTIMONIES, TEACHINGS AND MORE:

WEBSITE/BLOG: LEAHMARIECARSON.COM

PODCAST: LENS OF FAITH (ON ALL PLATFORMS)

INSTAGRAM: @LENSOFFAITH_

FACEBOOK PAGE AND GROUP: LENS OF FAITH

YOUTUBE + RUMBLE CHANNEL: LEAH MARIE CARSON

THANK YOU FOR THE LOVE

"It's one thing to say you believe the stories in the Bible but Leah is living a modern-day Bible story. Her incredible journey of faith and endurance is like the ones we talk about in churches and Bible studies."
-Deborah M.

"I couldn't put this book down! I was hanging on each word! Leah is proof of God. She so beautifully displays how Christ makes all things new when we surrender to him." -Karen A.

"The world will be impacted and set free by these words and Leah's uncompromising life of faith. She truly walks with God and is the real deal." -Pastor Marcus P.

"This powerful book will lead you to freedom and a deeper trust in Jesus." -Melissa M.

LEAH CARSON is founder of Lens of Faith® Ministries est. 2016. She is an entrepreneur, an influential writer, podcaster, speaker, content creator and activist who takes a bold stand for righteousness. Leah mentors women and is a living example of what God will do with a life that is truly surrendered.

LENS OF FAITH

LENS OF FAITH

Made in United States
Cleveland, OH
20 January 2025

13328349R00125